An Upward Climb Toward Faith

By

Jackie Phillips

For information regarding special discounts for bulk purchases, contact the publisher at Cjackiephillips@gmail.com.

Cover design and photography for cover by Christine Racz. Racz Photography, https://www.raczphotography.com/

Type design and typography by LT's Coaching & Educational Services, www.myfirstbook.org

Table of Contents

Dedication

This book is dedicated to my mother, Alice Jackson Kellogg, who went to be with the Lord over twenty years ago. She was a wonderful, God fearing and dedicated mother who gave me a faith structure through all my growing up years by raising me in a church. I am sure she must have prayed for me while I waivered and left God for several years. I still have a vivid picture of her on her knees before going to bed having her own conversation with God. She would be thrilled to see this book. I have no idea if you can see a book from heaven, but Mom, this one is for you. Never discount the impact that your actions have on your children. They are silently watching all that you do.

Endorsements

"What a beautifully written book. I am so grateful for the advantage I have over the million others who will read this book. Knowing you personally, I heard your voice in my head as I read it. At one point, you made me laugh out loud. What an honor to be able to be one of the first to be blessed by this book."

-Rohnda Bank, *Children' s Women's Ministry Pastor, Extreme Life Ministries*

"Jackie's "Upward Climb toward Faith," is filled with the spirit of One who has not just walked her journey, but run it by marathon, extracting the most of lives possibilities. Through her authenticity and the sharing of her story, with its Highs as well as the Lows (learning to let go of control) is beautifully told, engendering hope and faith; including the deeper understanding that our Upward Climb toward Faith is not about perfection. Yet, the willingness to stop long enough to "listen-in," and have the courage to answer the call with intentional action. The power of surrender, whereby facilitating an ease in comprehending that in "the midst," we have never been alone (but all-one), and its merit bringing forth Peace and Joy, living life as Blessing. As we halt in order to listen, assignments are given, and as we *ask* for Gods help, life flows in a more trusting and congruent fashion. From the heart, together with God-confidence in its wisdom, -- nothing seems impossible. When we do, as she shares in the chapter on Grace, life takes on a richer meaning, and our assignments flow to and through us, but not forced by us. Risen, in having felt God's Grace, despite our imperfections, savoring life, but not as a race; honing our talents given in service of others, empowering us with greater capacity to love our neighbors, as have become to love ourselves."

-Daniela Bumann, Bestselling Author, Motivational Speaker, Liberator, Life and Performance Coach, Corporate Consultant

"The introduction has you hooked! A book that one can relate to in our ongoing struggles with growing and practicing our faith in God and giving our lives totally to him. You learn, 'You Are Not Alone!'"

-Ellen Croswell Morrison, Member, *An Upward Climb toward Faith, Facebook Group*

"The book is good. I loved reading it. I think this will relate to my kids. I want them to read your book. All of them! I'm buying each a copy. "

-Kathy Dyer, *CEO Dyer Enterprises, Inc.*

"No matter where you are in your faith journey, whether you are at the beginning of your journey or well along the way, *An Upward Climb Toward Faith* is a book that will speak to you in some way. The chapter on Grace was the one that spoke to me the most. Read the book, you will find it inspirational, challenging and beautiful."

-Barbara Fenters, *Member of An Upward Climb toward Faith, Facebook Group*

"In *An Upward Climb Toward Faith*, author Jackie Phillips shares a beautiful and relatable "climb" to those of us who've felt led or called to do more... yet may not have always follow the prompt. Falling short everyday myself, but being the recipient of God's immeasurable Grace, helps me to recognize how special (and personal) this book is. Reading about Jackie's challenges and triumphs on her journey is inspirational.

-Kelli Holmes, *Founder and CEO, Team Referral Network*
www.teamreferralnetwork.com

"Jackie Phillips possesses the practical wisdom of Solomon and the relentless, encouraging spirit of Barnabas. She generously employs both traits to their full effect in *An Upward Climb toward Faith*. Long after the gossamer words have floated down from our pulpits and dissipated, someone needs to be there to share a cup of tea, roll up her sleeves, and say "here's how it really works." This marvelous book is Christian witness at its finest: making the grace and love of God accessible and real. I heartily recommend it to those who have been climbing for a while, are just getting started, or are still just thinking about it…it will bless you!"

-Reverend Bill Johnson, Pastor United Methodist Church

"Jackie Phillips wants your life to be filled with unspeakable joy, with faith in Jesus as the crux of the matter. Her compilation of devotionals covering everything from forgiveness to self-control could make a great contribution to that goal for your life."

-Randy W. Kirk, *Amazon Best Selling Author,*
SoCalMasterMInds.com

"A gentle nudge or a push? I've experienced both on my faith journey and appreciated how the author shared the downs and ups of her personal journey through the lens of God's infinite grace. The definition of faith is "complete trust or confidence in someone or something" – and in this case utter trust in God. Whether you've ever struggled, found it easy to be obedient, or lost your way, this book is a must-read to strengthen your faith as you make life decisions and seek to be being a blessing to others."

– Lisa Marie Platske, #1 International Best-Selling Author in 5 countries, *Turn Possibilities into Realities – From Fear to Faith*

"*An Upward Climb to Faith* provides an honest accounting of one woman's journey with the Lord. Jackie brings us along as she shares how the love of God inspires her to continue to run, walk, and sometimes crawl the upward race of faith. You will laugh, cry and see the power of the Holy Spirit at work transforming, encouraging, pushing her along the way. You will also recognize sacred moments in your own life and be inspired to continue your own walk of faith. An absolute joy to read."

-Rev. Melissa Rusler, Fallbrook United Methodist Church

"Jackie Phillips bares her soul with an uncommon depth of authenticity. Her story is a treasure, gently exemplifying the realities of how, even Christians at times, do struggle and even falter as they learn and grow in their faith. I feel better about being an ordinary human with faults and doubts having read it. This book is sure to bolster your personal hope in the Lord."

-Assunta Maria Vickers, Editor, Inland Empire California Writers Club *Fresh Ink.*

"For the Christian believer and the "seeker", this book will challenge you on your faith journey to continue to fight the good fight. We all fall short of the glory of God. Jackie shares her poignant faith journey providing inspiration, hope, joy, and what it means to live with God's ultimate grace and love which is a gift to everyone. *"An Upward Climb"* is a must have in your book collection and reminds us with faith anything is possible."

-Kristin Wertz Burrows, Corporate America Marketing Professional

Acknowledgements

Whew! Where to begin? This is probably the most difficult page to write. So many people have encouraged me in the writing of this book in so many ways. If you are one of those people, thank you from the bottom of my heart. There are, however, a few who deserve special recognition.

First and foremost, I want to say thank you to my Lord and savior, Jesus Christ, who is the head of my life. Without him, I would not be where I am today.

Secondly, I want to say thank you to my awesome and amazing Book Coach, Latasha Jimerson. Latasha served as a proofreader for my last book, and I knew we had a special connection. She gave me her all, her expertise, patience, time, and love as we went through this manuscript word by word and page by page, and finally sent it off to be printed.

Thanks to my kind and patient husband, Dick Phillips, who put up with me while writing yet another book and then proofread the final copy. Thank you so much Nikki Dewispelaere who is my wonderful daughter and proofreader. Barbara Fenters and Rohnda Banks also proofread this book before it was published.

Thank you so much Judy Johnson and Melissa Rusler, who have been my running and prayer partners for many years. These ladies have always encouraged me and prayed with and for me. Thank you, Judy, for also writing a wonderful Foreword for this book.

I want to give a special thanks to Rev. Bill Johnson, who is a friend of long standing and supported me in reaching a decision to follow Christ and mentored me as a new Christian.

Thank you Cindie Wertz for your faith during a tragic time. You truly helped us restore our faith. In addition, I also want to thank the Members of my amazing Facebook Group. The group is called, "An Upward Climb toward Faith." This group of awesome people made suggestions about content.

I also want to send a shout out to Assunta Vickers, too, who encouraged me to join the IE Chapter of the California Writer's Club.

Additionally, I want to thank my photographer Christine Racz. The Mt. Rubidoux picture on the cover and the entire cover was photographed and designed by Christine Racz, Racz Photography, Riverside, CA. Christine is a talented professional and friend who climbed to the top of Mt. Rubidoux to do these photo shoots with me.

Foreword

Even youths grow tired and weary,
and young men stumble and fall;
but those who hope in the LORD
will renew their strength.
They will soar on wings like eagles;
they will run and not grow weary,
they will walk and not be faint.[1]

Jackie Phillips and I were praying together at the onset of our first great adventure – a mini-triathlon at Green Valley Lake – and this was the guiding Scripture that the Holy Spirit put on my heart as we leapt out into the chilly mountain waters. This promise from Isaiah is the embodiment of Jackie's spirit…running, renewing, soaring!

I met Jackie at the Moreno Valley United Methodist Church in 1986 and I knew that my life would be forever changed. Jackie is not just a person that runs up immediately to a new face with a smile and a warm hand extended (although she is that). But Jackie is mostly a force of nature that changes the entire shape of the room and fills every corner with a radiance and a sense of welcoming. She has an expansive quality that wraps her arms around every person within her orbit. You know that when Jackie arrives, she is 'taking names' –but in a good way!

And yet, Jackie also possesses a quality of deep, intimate belonging as she leans into a quiet conversation and listens intently in that same crowded space that says, 'You are the most important person in my life right now and I am here for you.'

In this book, Jackie dismantles one of the most stubborn Christian heresies: the idea that there is any part of our lives that is secular, untouched by and disconnected from

---

[1] *Life Application Study Bible, New International Version,* Isaiah 40:30,31.

the real sacred work of worship and prayer. There is a tendency to speak of the sanctuary as somehow of more importance to God than the workplace, the home, the running trail…but not for Jackie. Jackie bursts forth in her life and in this book with stories about the ordinary becoming extraordinary. Jackie finds God in her daily life as the one wrapping His 'big ol' arms' around every person and dedicating them all to His glory. Jackie knows that our moments of exaltation and our stifled yawns somehow go together, part of the whole life we are meant to offer to God day by day, Sunday by Sunday. It is the life that Christ himself assumed, and therefore rescued and redeemed. Taste and see that the Lord is good. Take Jackie's hand through this book and find that every square inch of our lives, every second, is His.

Not unlike her infectious laugh, Jackie's life is an effervescent pool of living water that speaks to her testimony in Christ. It is not always easy, but it is steady. And when Jackie stumbles and is lifted again by the hand of God, her other hand is always extended to the next person on the climb. "I've been on this mountain before", she confides, "And I know the way up." Well done, good and faithful servant!

Dr. Judy Johnson, LEP, ABSNP

Asst. Professor, School Counseling/School Psychology
LPCC Clinical Counseling Coordinator
Azusa Pacific University
Soli Deo Gloria

Introduction

"I do not understand what I do.
For what I want to do I do not do, but what I hate, I do."
-Apostle Paul, Romans 7:15[2]

Let's begin with a disclaimer. On a walk, listening to praise music, I heard a whisper in my soul saying, "write my book!" Not being very skilled at listening to the promptings of the Holy Spirit, I thought, "what could I possible write about? "

You see, only one year earlier, I had just finished launching and promoting my first solo book project. The name of that book is *Step by Step: 21 Ways to Enhance the Winner in You*, and figured I was done with writing. Then the thought came that I should write a book about the things I wished I could do consistently, as a follower of Jesus Christ.

Just like Paul said in the book of Romans, the things I want to do, I do not always do. I remembered that scripture and immediately went home. Next, I wrote in my journal the topics which are the chapters of this book. Surprisingly, those thoughts flowed to me and through me, with minimal effort.

You would think that I immediately began, but that was not the case. Being the obedient person that I am *not*, those topics rested in my journal with few glances for over nine months!

---

[2] *Holy Bible,* Zondervan and Tyndale House Publishers, New International Version, 1984, Romans 7:15

Then, again, as I was walking, I heard a gentle whisper inside my spirit saying, "write my book!" This is all to say, that personally I do not get all these things perfect or even right, most of the time. Why is it that I do not always do what I want to do?

We all struggle, as evidenced by this famous quote, written to begin this chapter and the topic of this book, from the Apostle Paul, almost 2,000 years ago. Before Paul, there was a Psalmist, whose words date back to over 2,500 years. Although, there has been many debates about the identity of the author, this is the longest Psalm in the Bible and it has a powerful message.

In verse 36, the Psalmist says, "turn my heart toward your statutes and not toward selfish gain." He asked God many times, to be able to follow God's word, God's laws and decrees, God's statutes, and God's commands. Then, he asks for help in following all of these. He follows all those requests and says, "that I will not be put to shame." [3]

I think most of us have the best of intentions, but we do not always carry them out. Sometimes we feel ashamed because we are disobedient. We are blatantly aware of not doing what we know we are supposed to do. Other times, we are just clueless and focused on going our own way, not even listening to the promptings of the Holy Spirit.

---

[3] *Ibid*, Psalm 119:36

I get a lot of hope in my own struggle when I read the words of both the Psalmist and Paul. Both struggled. To me, following God's word is a constant journey of some steps forward, and just as many steps back. It is always an upward climb. This has been written to highlight what I wish I could always do. This book is not about what I have always done or do now. For me it has been an upward climb, hence the title of this book.

This is not a book of heavy-duty doctrine, but a book from a person who has searched and struggled and still does not have all the answers. Some days my faith is strong, and others it falters. This is not a how-to manual, but rather, a guide that says, "wouldn't it be great if we could always do what we want to do, which are the right things to do?"

Another question that I want to present to you is "imagine how amazing it would be for a person to honor what they believe God has called them to do? Although humans stumble and fall, we must keep striving to do our best. I believe God honors those attempts, feeble as they might be sometimes. I wrote this to give you hope.

This is written for the believer who sometimes doubts their own ability to do what is right. This is also for the person who is still searching, from a person who is an experienced Christian yet is still searching for answers. Wherever you are in your faith, know that there is a God who loves you greatly. He created you in his own image. He sacrificed his only son for you, and has infinite patience with you and me, and all his children.

We do not have to get it all right, because God knows our imperfections. Even with all those imperfections, he loves us anyway. That is the greatest story ever told. God is full of his grace for us. Now is the perfect time to explore the idea of grace and what it means for you, the seeker.

Grace

"Grace is God's best idea. His decision to ravage a people by love, to rescue passionately, and to restore justly - what rivals it? Of all his wondrous works, grace, in my estimation, is the magnum opus."
-Max Lucado[4]

A great place to begin when you think about *An Upward Climb to Faith* is God's amazing gift of grace. Grace is a word that you hear bantered around, but what does it really mean? Simply defined, grace is God's unmerited favor. Grace is his goodness toward those who have no claim on, nor reason to expect, divine favor.

Let me tell you. That would be you and me. The principal manifestation of God's grace has been in the form of a gift. Salvation is not our achievement, but it is a gift from God. He created each of us with a purpose in mind. Here is the unbelievable part, the God of the universe wants to have a relationship with us!

God has been very patient with me because it took me over 40 years to learn this lesson. Growing up, my faithful mother took me to a local Presbyterian church every Sunday. She was a woman who spent every night on her knees before she went to bed, a lesson I never quite learned.

---

[4]https://www.wow4u.com/godsgracequotes/

I grew up spending time in church, believed in God but never quite understood that God wanted to have a relationship with me! When I was in college, I figured I could do everything on my own. I stopped going to church and believed it was all up to me. My transition into college was smooth and I was successful living on my own. Therefore, I thought I did not need God anymore. I accomplished quite a bit and thought I had done everything "all on my own." Moreover, I worked hard and partied hard, too.

I married my college sweetheart who had also been raised in the church but also did not have a relationship with God. He joined the Air Force and flew fighter jets. He flew in the Vietnam war with 167 missions over enemy territory. After he returned, we continued just living for today, partied hard, and tried not to think about tomorrow. Every weekend we drank our share of alcohol and had a great time being young and carefree.

After being married for 12 years, we realized that we were living a self-centered lifestyle with too much partying and drinking booze. One year we got stationed in Germany. Neither of us had any relationship with the Lord. The word to describe my relationship with God was indifferent. We were not doing "evil" deeds; but sinful deeds that pushed us far away from God.

We wanted children badly at this time in our lives. Unfortunately, we tried to have children on our own and were unsuccessful. We even tried artificial insemination, but that did not work either. We also attempted to adopt a child before we moved to Germany but had to leave suddenly before our name came up on the list.

In Germany, we started, again, the adoption process to adopt a child born to U.S. servicewomen living overseas. Once, again, we became discouraged because the process was painfully slow. Even though we were not paying attention to God, he had a different plan for us for how we would become parents, but somehow, he had to get our attention.

Looking back over my life experiences, I have learned that I can be impatient and stubborn. At times, these qualities have served me well in dealing with humans, but not with God. As a driven, goal-seeking person, I used to be more focused on my results than people. My agenda was always to get what I wanted. I was a control freak.

In my thirties, things were pretty much going as I expected, and I felt no need for God. I had broken my leg badly and managed to go through a lot of grueling physical therapy. Because a "kind" Army doctor told me I could never run, again, I stubbornly began to run. The more I thought about what he said, the more determined I became to prove him wrong. Today, I am eternally grateful to that doctor, because 40 years later, I am still running.

Now is a good time to mention a time when life took over and my husband and I realized that we had no control over circumstances that shift our lives. One day, we got an unexpected phone call from the Air Force. The voice on the phone told us that Dick's best friend, Mike, had been killed. Mike was involved in a routine training accident when his plane flew into a mountain at another airbase in Germany about 100 miles from us.

We immediately traveled to see his wife, Cindie, and her young daughters. The girls were only four and seven years old at the time. Since we were all living far from home and overseas, the Air Force asked Dick to accompany the family back to the States. We decided that I would fly back with them, too. In the following weeks, our hearts and minds stayed focused on Cindie. Just imagine how difficult it was to be living so far from family and having your spouse killed!

Even writing this over 40 years later, I still get teary-eyed thinking about the day we got that phone call. I remember it vividly. It is odd how when painful things happen in your life, you remember exactly where you were and what you were doing at the time.

I remember that I was swimming in an indoor pool in our small town in Zweibruecken, Germany. The lifeguard signaled me to come to the side and said I had a phone call. It was my husband calling to tell me to come home immediately, so we could go see Cindie.

Cindie had so many decisions to make so quickly. Where should she go? Where should she bury Mike? Where would she and the girls live? Finally, after a week or so, we flew to Tulsa with Cindie and her girls where Mike's parents lived, and Mike was buried there. After spending 3 weeks with them, we returned to Germany to finish Dick's tour of duty. While we were with Cindie, we were touched and amazed by her faith at every turn. Watching her, we realized we were missing something crucial in our lives.

Upon our return to Germany, we started going to church again. That was something we had never done as a couple. A month later, late in October 1977, the Lord blessed us with a *good* phone call.

This good phone call was from the adoption agency saying that they had a little girl for us. We were so happy to have new baby girl. We have always told her that she was a blessing from God. Also, we decided to give her the middle name Michelle, which is after Mike, our friend who was killed in the training accident. She was and is still our only child. Of course, we were incredibly grateful and gave the credit to the Lord, but something crucial was *still* missing from our lives.

When we moved from Germany to Louisiana, and we decided to join a local Methodist church. The problem was that I was just sort of going through the church motions. I was back to being like that same kid who just spent time in church not really getting any kind of a connection.

I went to church, but I did not have a relationship with Christ. Life was better, but, again, something seemed to be missing. I wish I could say that I got the whole relationship thing correct, right away, but that was not the case. I am so thankful that God kept pursuing me. To be honest, God had to pursue me for another eleven years. I was just that stubborn.

Once again, Jesus interrupted my life in a powerful way. I was on an early morning hike up a mountain with a good friend of mine. This mountain is called Mt. Rubidoux and is in Riverside, CA. The cover of this book shows what it looks like to climb this mountain.

In December 1988, my friend and I saw a magnificent sunrise. Out of nowhere, my friend asked about my goals for the year. I went over them, and she asked' "so, when are you going to give up control, and give your life to Christ?"

Whew! Talk about a conversation stopper! She left me freezing to ponder that, and I spent a couple of hours at the top of that mountain arguing with God. We had climbed up a back way in the dark and by the time I was ready to leave, it was daylight.

I had difficulty finding a path to go down. It took me quite a while. I felt like Jacob wrestling with God. (Read the entire story in the book of Genesis.)[5]

---

[5] *NIV, Genesis,* 32; 22-32

With nothing still resolved I called my pastor, Bill Johnson, and he spent a good part of the day with me. After many cups of coffee at a local coffee shop, he asked if I would like to go to church and pray. I was reticent to give up my control, but, in that prayer, I finally did. Then I felt an unexplainable joy.

That joy still resides in me today. Now, rather than looking at people as an interruption and going my own way, I love being with people. I love to share the joy that I still have. I love to give others an encouraging word. None of that feels like a duty but now it brings me great fulfillment.

That, my friend, is God's grace. He pursued me even when I did not think I had a use for him. Undeserving as I was, he pursued me for many years. What a patient, forgiving, loving God he is; filled with grace. This grace is available to all who seek it. No matter where you are or what you have done, all you must do is seek him, acknowledge him, and ask for forgiveness.

Think of the final scene as Jesus hangs on the cross. What does Jesus do? In his last act as a man, he forgives. In a last-ditch effort, the criminal hanging next to Jesus said to Jesus, "remember me when you come into your kingdom." What does Jesus do? He says "truly I tell you that today you will be with me in Paradise.[6] This is grace.

---

[6] *NIV,* Luke 23:42-43

The song, *Amazing Grace*, is one of the most well-known songs ever. The author, John Newton, was a vulgar sea captain engaging in the Atlantic slave trade in the 1700s. He was constantly bad-mouthing Christians. On a voyage, he had a near-death experience when the ship he was on encountered a violent storm prompting him to cry out to the Lord. His ship and its crew were saved from disaster.

Years later, he left the sea and slave trafficking and started speaking out against slavery. Then, as an Anglican priest, he penned these lines as a poem, "amazing grace, how sweet the sound that saved a wretch like me. I once was lost, but now I am found, I was blind but now I see." Just like me, it took John Newton several years to "get it," but God never gave up.

The amazing part of the story is not his conversion, but that God kept pursuing him. This, my friends, is grace. In his famous ode, the Hound of Heaven, [7]Francis Thompson centers on the relentless pursuit of a sinner by a loving God. This poem is written in a style that is difficult to understand, but I love the visual image of a bloodhound relentlessly going after its mark and not giving up until it has found it.

---

[7]Nicholson, Thomas, "The Hound of Heaven," *The Oxford Book of English Mystical Verse*, Nicholson & Lee, eds. 1917.

That is our God. He relentlessly pursued me even when I thought I had no use for him, and he is relentlessly pursuing you. When will you submit to him and confess him as your Savior? Trust me, it is not as scary as you might think.

I was at a retreat in the fall of 2019, and a song really impacted me. The name of the song is the "The Goodness of God."[8] The song tells of how faithful God has been. The chorus struck me as so true for my own life. Even when I was far from God, he was still faithful and pursuing me. The chorus says, "cause all my life you have been faithful and all my life you have been so, so good." It sings of all the ways God has been faithful and the bridge is about God pursuing you and me, running after us. God does not just pursue us. He chases us.

As we have been given this fabulous gift of grace by the creator of the universe, should we do any less than to give grace to others? That is so much easier said than done. It is a constant struggle to give to others the same treatment that we would like to be given when we mess up. It is so much easier to be critical of others than to see our own faults.

Grace, however, is a two-way street. As we have been shown grace by our creator, we must constantly strive to give grace to others. This can all be summed up in the words of Jesus when asked what the greatest commandment was.

---

[8] Bethel Music and Johnson, Jenn, "The Goodness of God,"2019.

Jesus replied: "Love the Lord your God with all your heart and with all your soul and with all your mind. This is the first and greatest commandment. And the second is like it. 'Love your neighbor as yourself."[9]

This is not a suggestion. It is a commandment! Loving others means doing things for others, not for yourself. It means putting others first. As we have been given great unmerited grace, we must, in turn, return that same grace to others. Why is it a challenge? It is a challenge because people are not always loveable, and neither am I. We all make mistakes, but difficult as it is sometimes, we all need to give others the grace that we have been given.

---

[9] *NIV,* Matthew 22:37-38

Accountability

"It is not what we do, but also what we do not do for which we are accountable."
-John Baptiste Molier[10]

The popularity of being accountable might be just a notch above being disciplined. Both are something that we know we should do, but we do not want to do it. Why is that? Down deep, we all think we are awesome people. It is much easier for me to see what someone else is doing wrong than acknowledge my own wrongdoings.

Many of us (myself included) suffer from the sin of pride, and the idea of admitting our shortcomings to another is unsettling, to say the least. There are two types of accountability, one is to the Lord, and the other would be to a person or group of people. Somehow, it is easier for me to admit my shortcomings to the Lord than to another person. Why is that?

Again, it is our pride. It is a challenge from our vantage point to see what we are doing wrong. I love the Bible verse that says, "Why do you look at the speck of sawdust in other's eyes and pay no attention to the plank in your own eye?

How can you say to your brother, 'let me take the speck out of your eye,' when all the time there is a plank in your own eye?

---

[10] https://www.goalcast.com/2018/01/08/moliere-quotes

You hypocrite, first take the plank out of your own eye, and then you will see clearly to remove the plank from your brother's eye."[11] To get the plank out of our own eye, sometimes we must seek help to become aware of what our "plank" or blind spot is. Others can always see it more clearly than we can see it ourselves. Once we are aware of our blind spot, then we must be willing to change it and grow through it.

Bringing about change is extremely difficult. In my experience, I have only seen a few organizations that have been successful in helping people transform their lives for the better. Weight Watchers, Alcoholics Anonymous, and Teen Challenge, come to my mind. What do these organizations have in common?

Well, their members must be accountable for their actions. The leaders of the organizations have built-in accountability systems to support those who struggle with addictions and unhealthy lifestyles. Members get access to individual sponsors, counselors, and support groups to help them make permanent changes in their lives. Should Christians be accountable in their walk?

Just because we are Christians does not mean that we do not make mistakes. We frequently have blind spots that are a challenge for us to see, but they can be glaring to others.

---

[11] *TEV,* Matthew 7:3

We are not made to live a life without Christian brothers and sisters who hold us to our faith, and they care for us loving and correct us when they see us start to falter.

The book of Proverbs says, "As iron sharpens iron, so one person sharpens another."[12] If you want to get better at anything, it helps to surround yourself with people who are better than you. They help you to up your game.

As a runner, I always run faster when I run with a partner or I am entered in a race. There is just something about falling into pace with someone else. Solomon was known as the wisest man ever, Solomon, once said, "Two are better than one because they have a good return for their labor. If one falls, one can help the other up."[13]

Christian accountability can be found in all sorts of groups. Many churches offer a small group structure to help not only with fellowship but to provide an atmosphere of support. Bible study groups with discussions following also provide a forum to facilitate fellowship and support. People are even able to form a group for personal Bible study with an app called the Bible app.

For the past three years, I have been involved in such a group taking 3 years to read the entire Bible. There is a daily check off the chapter to be read and an opportunity to share with the group. There is also an accountability app for phones.

---

[12] NIV, Proverbs 27:17
[13] Ibid, Ecclesiastes 4:9-10

The years I grew most in my faith was when I was a part of an accountability group called "Covenant Disciple." It was through my Methodist church, and eight of us, both men and women, met every Sunday to do a check-up on ten actions. Those areas were acts of compassion, justice, devotion, and worship. We agreed to do those actions on a daily or weekly basis. We decided as a group what those ten actions would be. The actions we agreed to were:

1. Express genuine appreciation to at least one person each day.
2. Have a meaningful conversation with at least one family member each week.
3. Stand up for those who are not present or able to stand up for themselves.
4. Practice responsible stewardship of the world's resources and my own body.
5. Read the Bible daily.
6. Pray each day for someone else, including members of the covenant disciple group.
7. Pray for those who lead us in worship and those who will visit us to be touched by grace.
8. Worship each Sunday.
9. Obey the promptings of the Holy Spirit to serve God and my neighbor.
10. Recognize the warning of the Holy Spirit when my words should remain unspoken.

Those ten actions were easy to measure, as to whether we had done them or not. At first, we all struggled with spiritual promptings. (That is when you get a feeling that you should or should not do something.) As we gathered week by week, we got better at recognizing those promptings. By listening as others shared, we got better at discovering our own promptings.

This group worked very well for me. However, you might do better with a spiritual coach or mentor. That is a person of the same gender whom you feel is further along the road, spiritually, than you. If you choose a spiritual mentor, you must also be willing to take their counsel.

Whether you choose an individual or a group, you must have two important elements: trust, and the ability to relate. Developing trust is a slow process, and it takes time to develop and grow. As people meet to share, they begin to establish rapport with one another.

To be accountable, one must be willing to open up and be vulnerable. To do this, there must be trust. Relating is an important factor in Christian accountability. It is helpful when the group shares a common bond or has been through similar experiences. People who can relate to one another have empathy with one another.

As stated, as we began this chapter, being accountable to another person or persons is only part of the accountability challenge. We must also be accountable to God.

That accountability can be called spiritual formation or just being formed in the Spirit. In the many years we spent in the Methodist church, we learned to admire its founder, John Wesley. All his life, John rose early and spent time with the Lord.

John was a pioneer in creating methods (hence the name Methodist) for believers to do a check-up on their spirituality. These have been called the means of grace and they are prayer, searching scripture, receiving the Lord's supper, fasting, and conferencing.

John based much of the Methodist movement on these five means that God uses to draw us closer to Him. Much has been written about these. One book, by Elaine A. Heath, *Five Means of Grace,*[14] gives the details of these means.

In addition, John came up with 21 questions for personal accountability. These questions plus more from other theologians can be found in the article from *Christianity Today.*[15] Whether you decide on a group or a mentor, it is imperative to establish the criteria before beginning.

Suffice it to say that to have spiritual growth, we need a plan. That plan depends upon the individual, but without a plan, spiritual growth will not happen.

---

[14] Heath, Elaine, *Five Means of Grace,* Abingdon Press, Nashville, TN, 2017
[15] https://www.christianitytoday.com/edstetzer/2008/may/accountability-questions.html

As I look back on my life, I can see that when I had a plan in place, I was much more successful. When I had no plan, I floundered. When I get off track, I must go back to some plan.

As I was writing this chapter, I realized that I was floundering, AGAIN. That means getting back to a plan. As I typed those ten covenant acts, I was struck by wondering why I had given up on those. I decided that could be my plan. Isn't it great how God reminds you of what you need to do? Hopefully, as I finish this book, I will be back on track, again!

Confess

"God removes the sin of the one who makes humble confession, and thereby the devil loses the sovereignty he had over the human heart."
--- Saint Bernard---[16]

When we invite Jesus into our lives, we first need to admit that we are sinners in need of a savior. Our next step is to confess our sin and accept him as our savior. To do that, we need to have a clear definition of sin. Simply stated, sin is anything that separates us from God. Somehow, we get hung up on what I am going to call *"big"* sin (murder, adultery, idolatry, robbery, to mention a few) and *"little"* sin (gossip, anger, jealousy, envy, an unforgiving heart, etc.). To God there is no difference. It all separates us from Him.

For me personally, it is a constant struggle to recognize what I am going to call the "little sin." The big ones are easy to recognize, but the small ones are more subtle.

I am not very introspective. I tend to always focus on the positive, and I am not the best at recognizing what I am doing to break God's heart. That is why it is so important to be in groups with others. Often by conversing with others I begin to see my own shortcomings. I appreciate my church leaders helping us to see our shortcomings.

---

[16]www.picturequotes.com/god-removes-the-sin-of-the-one-who-makes-humble-confession-and-thereby-the-devil-loses-the-quote-928229

In the letter to the Romans, Paul states, "for all have sinned and fall short of the glory of God."[17] How much clearer can that get? **ALL** have sinned. That certainly does mean both you and me. If we are all in the same boat, what can be done about it? Furthermore, is there a penalty? Again, we go to Paul's letter to the Romans, "For the wages of sin is death, but the gift of God is eternal life in Jesus Christ our Lord."[18] Before we get all hung up on the death penalty, let us see what that really means. It is a spiritual death rather than a physical one. Spiritual death is a separation from God. If sin separates us from God, how do we get back to a right relationship with him?

The answer is that we have a choice to simply confess and ask for forgiveness. One of my favorite bumper stickers says, "I am a Christian, not perfect, but forgiven." Once we have asked for forgiveness, what guarantee is there that forgiveness will be given? The apostle John gives us that assurance saying, "If we confess our sins, he is faithful and just to forgive us our sins and to purify us from all unrighteousness."[19] Then, the slate is wiped clean. God does not even remember the sin. We have a fresh start. However, there is a responsibility that we will not continue that *particular* sin.

---

[17] NIV, Romans 3:23
[18] *NIV*, Romans 6:23
[19] *Ibid.* 1 John 1:9

Confession is a part of the accountability mentioned in the last chapter. Our all-knowing God knows of our wrongdoings. He even knows the things in our minds that we have thought about, but not yet done. In the book of Hebrews, the author states, "There is nothing that can be hidden from God; everything in all creation is exposed and lies open before his eyes. And it is to him that we must all give an account of ourselves."[20]

Confessing our sins gives us the opportunity to admit when we are wrong, not only to God, but to ourselves. We cannot fix what we do not first acknowledge. Once a Christian has acknowledged sin, they are free to ask God for forgiveness. That is one aspect. The other then is asking for forgiveness if a person has wronged another.

Confession also takes away the power to keep us locked in our sin by the devil. The devil can cause a feeling of guilt that what we have done will not be forgiven by God. We can be easily led astray to believe that we are not worthy of forgiveness. Have you ever heard someone say something to the effect that what they have done is so bad that it is unforgivable? Once our sin is out in the open, it loses its hold over us.

---

[20] Ibid, Hebrews 4:13

All this sounds easy until you have to do it. However, saying, "I am sorry," is incredibly challenging for most of us. It makes us feel vulnerable. While writing this, I decided to Google "Why is it so hard to say, I'm sorry?" I was astounded by the results. There were over 800,000 results to this question. This said to me that I am not the only one who struggles with this. It is a prevalent struggle for many of us.

Why is it so difficult to say I am sorry? The small things are not as much of a problem as the bigger issues. Once I realize and recognize that I have wronged someone, (which is another issue) I can say I am sorry to people I have knowingly wronged. However, when I end up looking bad it is not so easy. My tendency is to go crashing around in my own little world not focusing on others. I hurt others unintentionally by being obsessed with my own agenda. Taking my eyes off my own agenda and considering the needs of others; that is my personal challenge.

Confession is just one part of a Christian's prayer life. There are three others, and there is a four-part acronym that teaches us how to pray. It is ACTS. The A is Adoration (worship of God); the C is Confess, the T is Thanksgiving (thanking God for our many blessings) and the S is Supplication (prayers for others). From looking at this acronym, it is apparent that confessing is to be a major part of our prayer life.

Why should it be a major part of our prayer life? By confessing, we are acknowledging our sin. God already knows what we have done wrong but confessing helps us to see where we have not been obedient and gives us the opportunity to make amends. Sometimes just confessing clears the air.

What should be confessed? We should confess anything that breaks God's laws and does not honor him. That would include three aspects: our thoughts, our words, and our actions. Personally, sometimes, I catch my brain in mid-stream when I realize that I am thinking negative thoughts about someone. Then I need to confess what I am doing and take those thoughts away. I have trained myself to intentionally "press the STOP button" on those nasty thoughts roaming around in my head.

What about grumbling? Have you ever grumbled to yourself? I know I have. It was brought to my attention by a sermon highlighting the travels of the Israelites through the wilderness complaining about the lack of food and water.[21] While these were real needs, nothing could be accomplished by complaining. Prayer would have been a much better plan. I realized that I try not to say things I know I should not say out loud, but that does not stop me from thinking them. I had never thought of grumbling in your head as a sin.

---

[21] Ibid, Exodus, Chapters 16 and 17

Here, again, followers of Christ must make a conscious effort to confess that behavior, and then stop grumbling and pray. Whether we are grumbling in our heads or out loud or just plain missing the mark of what God would have us do, confession is necessary to strengthen our relationship with the Lord.

I heard a great story from a good friend who is a Realtor about just how freeing it can be to confess your thoughts and ask for forgiveness. I am going to call her Jane. She had a disagreement with a client who treated her very unfairly. She did everything to sell the client's high value home, and the client was still not happy. The client blamed Jane and turned down a fair offer based on the suggested sales price. The client hurt Jane, and Jane ended up losing the sale. The house was relisted with another agent who also listed another high value home of that client. Jane was so hurt by her client who was also a friend, that she got counseling. After counseling with pastors and her husband, she vowed to let this hurt go and give it to God.

Letting go was easier said than done, though. Wanting to see what happened on the sale of the house, Jane put the home on her watch list, so she could spy on them. This spying was sinning, because she had vowed to just let it go. She heard from God clearly, "Jane, take those homes off the watch list; you can leave that in the past."

On a walk with her husband, she confessed to her husband that she had spied on the other agent and told her husband how God had spoken to her. Her husband then reminded her of all the blessings they had received from the Lord and told her to stop spying.

When they returned home from the walk, there was a box on the front door. It was from the person, named Pam, who had led Jane to the Lord. Pam had also given Jane her first Bible at the age of 17. In that Bible, Jeremiah 29:11 was underlined, "For I know the plans I have for you, declares the Lord; plans to prosper you and not to harm you, plans to give you a future and hope." [22] The box on the porch contained a book that Pam had authored. In the book, she mentioned Jane as the first person to whom she had witnessed. To quote my friend Jane, "How awesome it was to see God show up at my front door to remind me of Jeremiah 29:11. When I felt alone and hurt and confessed to my husband, I got a confirmation that God had heard me." In addition to our thoughts, we also need to confess our words. Sometimes, I do not control those nasty thoughts. They automatically pop out of my mouth. Then my anger, my gossip, my slander, or anything else that is not uplifting comes to the forefront and out of my mouth. Then I must confess not only to the Lord but apologize to the person whom I have offended.

---

[22] *NIV,* Jeremiah 29:11

Lastly, we Christians need to confess our actions. What have we done to be disobedient? I may get a gut feeling that I should or should not do something. When I ignore that feeling, which is actually a prompting from the Holy Spirit, I am being disobedient. I am particularly adept at rationalizing that disobedience. A great example for me was the feeling I felt when I realized I was supposed to write *this book*.

Oh yes, I rationalized. I had just finished another book. I was tired of writing, blah, blah, blah. I was just being disobedient, plain, and simple. I could just say I was sorry, but that would not solve it. Once we confess, then we have to stop doing (or not doing) whatever is separating us from God. For me, I had to stop procrastinating on writing this book. For my friend Jane, she had to stop spying on the home for sale.

Encouragement

"Therefore, encourage one another and build each other up, just as in fact you are doing."
-Apostle Paul[23]

This quote became real to me almost 20 years ago, when I was running my first marathon. My friend, Melissa, and I had tried for several years to run a marathon, but something kept sidetracking us before we could complete the training. Between the two of us, we suffered from: a torn rotator cuff, a torn hamstring, and breast cancer.

Despite these obstacles, we were eventually able to finish six months of training. We were right on track and had just completed a 22-mile run. We were starting to taper our runs. That means, we started to decrease the distance running to rest more.

Nineteen days before the race, I had severe abdominal cramping and felt terribly ill. I headed to the emergency room late on New Year's Day. I do not think it was a coincidence that the doctor assigned to me was a marathoner. He told me that I needed an emergency appendectomy. I was in tears and told him about my marathon plans.

---

[23] NIV, I Thessalonians 5:11

Rather than tell me I could not run the marathon, he told me that he thought I could. I had a full surgery with a 3-inch incision. My post-operative instructions were no running, driving, or showering for 10 days post-surgery.

Then, I was to run 10 miles with a back brace around my abdomen and come in for my post-operative exam. I did that and he encouraged me and cleared me to run. Nine days later, off we went to Carlsbad, California, to run that marathon with a lot of people praying for us.

Running a marathon takes a lot of stamina. You build that up over a six-month period of time. However, at some point, almost every runner begins to wear down. It is such a phenomenon, there is a name for it. The name for that is, "hitting the wall."

When we first started to run the marathon, we were doing great for the first few miles. We had been covered in prayer, and I really did not have a lot of pain at my incision. We were even actually running faster than we thought we would. We had a group of friends and family at mile thirteen cheering and encouraging us.

Our husbands met us along the way and restocked us with energy foods and drinks. All was going great, until we passed the 20-mile mark. When I get tired, I throw my leg outward so that it looks very awkward to spectators. This is the same leg in which I ripped one third of my hamstring and it never completely healed.

Melissa can usually hear me dragging my leg and she tells me. I am unaware that I am doing it. Around mile twenty-two Melissa commented to me how great the endorphins were. I was really wearing down though and told her. She realized I was throwing my leg, again.

Just after that a man standing along the route yelled at me, "You are looking great!" I knew it was a lie, but he apparently saw I was having trouble and took the time to encourage me. His kind words encouraged me so that I was able to grit my teeth and finish those last four miles. That incident was many years ago, and I do not even remember what the man looked like. What I still remember is how his act of kindness impacted me in a big way.

That man will never know what he did for me that day. I can, however, tell you, his encouraging words did make a HUGE difference. Let that be a lesson for all of us, that we ALL have the power to be tremendous encouragers.

Running that marathon was an experience in encouragement that I will never forget. From the doctor that told me I could do it, to our friends and families, the people at the water stations, and just the strangers who lined the route, we were encouraged every step of the way. Right after that marathon, I found the verse that begins this chapter. I committed it to memory, and decided that it would be my life verse, one by which I try to live.

So how do we go about encouraging one another and building one another up? We first must decide that we will always do that and refrain from ever making a disparaging remark to another person. Since that is counter intuitive, we must ask for help from the Holy Spirit.

In a letter to the Romans, the apostle Paul talks about spiritual gifts and says, "If your gift is encouraging, then give encouragement."[24] That means that some of us have been given the gift of encouragement to build others up in the body of Christ. If that is you, then make certain to use it. If that is not you, then ask for help in learning to use it.

We need to be encouraging in two ways: 1) we always need to be edifying in all that we say and 2) we need to guard against all disparaging remarks that we make about others (gossip). Making encouraging remarks is a habit and once formed, it becomes second nature.

As fragile humans we must focus on elevating and encouraging others. I wrote a whole chapter on this in my book, *Step by Step, 21 Steps to Enhance the Winner is You.* [25] Stopping gossip is more difficult. First, it is necessary to realize that it is happening. Once we become aware, then we must make a conscious decision to stop.

[24] *NIV,* Romans 12: 8
[25] Phillips, Jackie, *Step by Step, 21 Steps to Enhance the Winner in You,* Phillips Wellness Enterprises, 2019

There is an old adage taught to me by my mother, "If you can't say something nice, then don't say anything at all."

Our words have tremendous power; power to lift or power to hurt and wound. It takes some practice to become an encourager, but it is well worth the effort. You must look for what people are doing right and comment on this. With this practice, it soon becomes a skill and just a part of who you are.

I love this quote by Maya Angelou, because it illustrates my point, she says, "I've learned that people will forget what you said, people will forget what you did, but people will never forget how you made them feel."[26]

I am amazed at how few people take the time to just say hello to others. Since I made a commitment to do at least 15,000 steps a day, I am always out in my neighborhood either walking or running. Most times I am the first one to say hello to someone I am passing. I smile and say hi. If I see them several times, I stop and ask their name and try to remember it. Since I am not always successful at remembering a name, I ask them a second time. They are usually incredibly happy to tell me their name, again. Then, they admit that they forgot mine too. If it is an uncommon name, I often ask them to spell it for me.

---

[26] https://www.brainyquote.com/quotes/maya_angelou_392897

Since I am a visual learner, this strategy helps me visualizing what it looks like on paper, and then I remember their name. When we become an encourager of people, there is no place in our conversations for sarcasm.

The root of the word sarcasm is the cutting of flesh. Even though it is sometimes meant in jest, it literally can cut flesh and be very damaging to people. Humor should never be created at someone's expense.

Decide right now that you will always be an encourager to people. Then, commit to do the other half which to stop making ugly remarks about people. Also, refuse to participate when others begin to gossip about someone else. Walk away or say something to defend the person who is about to be maligned. It is so easy to get sucked into gossip.

Sometimes it happens before you are even aware of it. The book of Proverbs states, "Gossip is so tasty – how we love to swallow it." [27] If we compare gossip to a tasty chocolate treat, once we taste it, it becomes difficult to refuse more. Just like the dieter, the only way we can truly avoid it, is just not to start in the first place. Look back at the verse with which I began this chapter. Make your best effort to always be encouraging to everyone. When you fail, know you are not alone in this.

---

[27] *NIV,* Proverbs 18:8

Fruit of the Spirit

"Heavenly Father, I pray this day that I may live in your presence and please you more and more. Lord Jesus, I pray that this day I may take up my cross and follow you. Holy Spirit, I pray that this day you will fill me with yourself and cause your fruit to ripen in my life: love, joy, peace, patience, kindness, goodness, faithfulness, gentleness and self-control."
-John Stott[28]

Why do you suppose that Paul called the character traits that Christians can develop, the fruit of the Spirit? He states, "But the fruit of the Spirit is love, joy, peace, forbearance, kindness, goodness, faithfulness, gentleness, and self-control. Against such things, there is no law."[29] It is because fruit has to be cultivated. Cultivation is a process that does not occur in the blink of an eye.

According to the World Atlas, the tree that takes the longest to bear fruit is the pawpaw tree.[30] This tree takes from 5 to 7 years to bear fruit. Having never tasted the fruit from a pawpaw tree, I do not know if it is worth the wait. Many trees take from 3 - 7 years such as cherry, pear, plum, apple, apricot, persimmon, nectarine, and peach.

[28] Wright, Christopher, J.H, Cultivating the Fruit of the Spirit. InterVarsity Press, Oak Grove, IL, 2017, p. 13
[29] *NIV*, Galatians 5:22-23
[30] https://www.worldatlas.com/articles/trees-that-take-the-longest-to-fruit

During this time, there is little proof that much of anything is happening there. Yet the grower must tend to the tree by watering and fertilizing. This is an act of faith that the fruit will one day appear on the tree.

Once the fruit begins to appear, the tree must be pruned. Finally, after much attention, the fruit can be harvested at the proper time. We moved to a new home about three years ago and found an apricot tree in the garden. We had no idea when the tree had been planted, but there was no fruit the first year. The second year, there was fruit, but we were gone during the time it was bearing fruit and, again, we missed it.

This year, my husband patiently pruned the tree. We had a bounteous crop. One day, as I was trying to figure out what to do with all the fruit, birds attacked. Within 8 hours, those birds had knocked almost all our fruit off that tree. The lesson here is that cultivation is a process and sometimes things turn out differently than expected. Next year, I hope to get nice apricots and no birds to grab them. Our lives in the Lord are much like that. As we grow in Christian maturity, we grow more in the characteristics of Christ. All that does not happen without time and effort by us and the Lord. It is a process and should not be disturbed. The fruit of the Spirit are all characteristics of Christ given to us by his Spirit.

As we continue to grow in Christ and walk with Him, we ask for His help in maturing the seeds of these fruits. Those seeds were planted in us when we gave our lives to Christ.

Just like the growing fruit analogy, those seeds must be nourished (studying His word) watered (being nourished by His living water through prayer), and finally pruned (disciplined).

The prayer in the quote at the beginning of this section is by John Stott, a 21st-century Anglican priest, author, noted theologian, and evangelist. This was the prayer he offered each morning when he first woke up. It is said that he shaped the faith of a generation.[31] Many people who knew this man personally, said he was the most Christlike person they had ever met. Although he is now deceased, he is still influencing people's faith through his books. We hear him quoted or referred to by our pastors frequently.

How did he have such a huge impact? God answered his daily prayer by making the fruit of the spirit ripen in his life. In so doing, he impacted many lives and will continue to do so. We will take these 9 characteristics one by one, beginning with the first and foremost, love. (Whenever the word fruit is used in this manuscript it will be used as Paul used it in his quote in Galatians).

---

[31] Wright, Christopher, J.H, Cultivating the Fruit of the Spirit. InterVarsity Press, Oak Grove, IL, 2017

Love

"Jesus is the reason we even know what love is. In laying down his life for us, he taught us everything we need to know about true love. Love is self-sacrificing, generous, unending, not a temporary feeling or attraction. Because of God's love for the world, we know that love is also undeserving and often unreciprocated." [32]
-Kristi Walker

Of the nine kinds of fruit that the Spirit gives, the first listed is love. Why is that? Love is the underlying quality under which all others must fall. Without love it is not possible to have the other eight. Love must be all encompassing. What is this love? Why is it so essential? The quote above gives some of the qualities of love.

Unlike the romantic love that is touted in our secular lives, today, Christian love is agape love or Godly love. Unlike the definitions that society has today for love, agape love is almost indescribable. To understand the true meaning, we must look at what it is and what it is *not*. Probably the best definition is from the Apostle Paul in his famous letter to the Corinthians.

In this letter, Paul gives us a clearer idea of what love is. It is often used in wedding ceremonies. However, this is not meant to just be the love between two people but agape love.

---

[32] https://www.christianity.com/wiki/christian-terms/what-is-love.html

It would be a rare marriage in which all these aspects of love would be always practiced. Paul says, "Love is patient, love is kind. It does not envy, it does not boast, it is not proud. It does not dishonor others, it is not self-seeking, it is not easily angered, it keeps no records of wrong. Love does not delight in evil but rejoices with the truth. It always protects, always trusts, always hopes, always perseveres.[33]

How then are we supposed to love? We are supposed to love in two ways. Jesus gives us the answer in the Gospel of Matthew when asked what the greatest commandment is. He replied, "Love the Lord your God with all your heart and with all your soul and with all your mind. This is the first and greatest commandment. And the second is like it. Love your neighbor as yourself."[34]

First, we must love God with all our being. In her book, *In His Image,* on page 39, Jen Wilken talks about what the love of God looks like. She states, "It looks like the full deployment of our heart, soul, mind, and strength – the totality of our being – in the active love of God. Everything we think, say and do is for the glory of God."

---

[33] *NIV,* 1 Corinthians 13:4-7
[34] *NIV,* Matthew 22: 37-39

Second, we must love our neighbors as we love ourselves. The parable of the good Samaritan found in the Gospel of Luke does a fantastic job of telling us who our neighbor is.[35] Travelling along an ancient highway, a man is savagely beaten, stripped, robbed, and left to die.

Two men pass him by for one reason or another. The third, a Samaritan, (a hated group of people) stops, bandages the man's wounds, and takes him to an inn. There he cares for him and then pays the innkeeper for the man's additional stay. Truly this was an act of agape love.

At the time of this writing, (the end of 2020) our country is filled with anger, distrust, and hate. At no time in our history have we been so divided. With all this happening and social media becoming a place of nasty venting, it is hard to take the high road and love. As Christians, though, we must.

While not easy, we can learn to love others because God first loved us. The apostle John states, "We love because he first loved us."[36] Through his love, he gives us the power to love. We must decide every day to be people who are known for our love. To love, we must practice love and always show love to others. I am not saying it is easy. It is an exceedingly difficult process but one which can be learned.

---

[35] *Ibid,* Luke 10:30 – 37
[36] *Ibid,* 1 John 4:19

Love is a verb, and like any other skill we have to practice to get better at it. As we grow in our relationship with Christ, we will become more like him. In his book, *The Greatest Thing in the World*, author Henry Drummond likens our relationship to Christ as to a piece of iron placed in the presence of an electrified body. That piece of iron is changed into a magnet so long as it remains side by side in the presence of the permanent magnet. Drummond states, "Remain side by side with him who loved us, and you, too, will become a permanent magnet, a permanently attractive force; and like him you will draw all men unto you. That is the inevitable effect of love."[37] When we find it difficult to love, (and we will) we need to try harder. We need to ask the Holy Spirit to come to our aid and cling closely to the Lord. In doing so, we can discover that God is the source of all love. The apostle John states "Dear friends, let us love one another, for love comes from God. Everyone who loves has been born of God and knows God. Whoever does not love does not know God, because God is love.[38]

---

[37] Drummond, Henry, *The Greatest Thing in the World*, New York: Mt. Vernon, Peter Pauper Press, p. 42
[38] *NIV*, I John 4:7-8

When Christians love one another, it proves the reality of God. When Christians take on the hate or indifference of the world, it has the opposite effect. It is a good reality check to remember that you and I are the only picture of Christ some people may see. Therefore, it is imperative that we seek to love as we have been loved.

Joy

On that day when I gave up my control and turned my life over to Christ, I remember being filled with an unfathomable joy. I was almost giddy with my newfound commitment. Although, that super high feeling gradually went away, I remain a more joyful person to this day. It is not just happiness, but a deep, abiding sense of well-being. How can that be? Joy is a fruit of the spirit. As such, it is given freely.

What then is this joy? *Theopedia* defines it as, "Joy is a state of mind and an orientation of the heart. It is a settled state of contentment, confidence and hope." [40] According to Bill High, a great definition is given by Jon Piper, "Christian joy is a good feeling in the soul, produced by the Holy Spirit, as he causes us to see the beauty of Christ in the word and in the world."[41] The word joy or joyful is mentioned 242 times in the Bible. What then brings us joy? What makes our eyes sparkle? Joy is different for each of us.

[39] https://www.awakenthegreatnesswithin.com/35-inspirational-quotes-on-joy/
[40] https://www.theopedia.com/joy
[41] https://billhigh.com/faith/how-do-you-define-joy/

For me, there are many things, but these are the most important things in my life. Having a family, having faith, having a future, and the wind on my face.

Having a family – this is not just my immediate family. This includes friends and the family in Christ. That is not to say that my immediate family does not give me great joy. It is my absolute joy when our grandson rings the doorbell and then hides before we answer. He then jumps out at us and says "Boo!" Seeing him do something for the first time and watching him grow as he experiences success, brings me joy. I also experience joy when I hear a quiet, "I love you," from the people I love most. What could possibly replace a warm hug from someone close to me? Any of those shared experiences with the people whom we love, whether they are family or friends, put a smile in our hearts. There is a joy in belonging to the family of God through Jesus Christ. Whether you have a biological family or not, the family of God is available to all.

Having faith – sometimes I am filled with intense joy worshipping in church or praying with someone. Some days when I run or am driving and have praise music in my ear, I am just filled with total joy belting out a favorite song not caring how I sound. The word Gospel means good news. If you have received the Gospel and know Jesus, then you know the good news. This should fill us with joy. This joy is not dependent upon circumstances. God wants us to be joyful in all circumstances.

In John, Jesus tells us, "I have told you this so that my joy may be in you and that your joy may be complete."[42] I believe that Jesus was filled with joy when he walked on this earth. That inner joy was one thing that drew crowds of people to him. They could sense that something was different about this man. In the letter to the Philippians, Paul says, "Rejoice in the Lord, always. I will say it again, rejoice."[43]

---

[42] NIV, John 15:11
[43] NIV, Philippians 4:4

That brings us to the letter to the Philippians. This is called the joy letter. It calls on us to be joyful in all situations. This letter was written by the apostle Paul while he was imprisoned in Rome and chained to a Roman guard. If any person had a reason not to be joyful, it would have been Paul. Yet throughout this letter he stresses being joyful in all situations. We see that being exhibited in his life. Despite his circumstances, he was filled with the joy of the Lord.

Having a future – my heart is filled to overflowing when I think of what Jesus did for me. He endured mocking, beating, betrayal, and finally a horrible death on a cross to save me from my sins. He has promised that we will spend eternity together. That certainly gives me hope and joy. In the book, *The Fruit of the Spirit* by Thomas Trask and Wayde Goodall, they state, "Our greatest earthly pleasure is only a small touch of what we will experience in heaven's eternity. Our unique joy begins with the fact that Christ lives within us, we belong to him, we are eternally alive in him.
This joy the world can never understand. "[44]

---

[44] Trask, Thomas and Goodall, Wayde, *The Fruit of the Spirit,* Nashville, TN, 2000, p.39

The wind in my face – as I was thinking through this chapter and what brings me joy, this had to be mentioned. I grew up in Florida and had a small sailboat. I was frequently on the water feeling the wind in my face sailing. I still love all kinds of boats. Now, I love to ride personal watercraft. The first ride of the morning, when it is still a bit chilly, is really exhilarating. There is that slight chill and the wind in my face. It often makes me break into song.

I feel that same deep satisfaction riding my bike in the cool of the morning with that breeze on my face. For me, that is a deep joy at just being alive. These are all fine and good, but how do we go about finding God-given joy? Joy from the Lord is not dependent upon conditions. It is in our hearts. Working in squalid conditions in the slums of India, friends of Mother Teresa said that despite being overwhelmed by the suffering around her, she almost glowed with joy as she went about her ministry.

In the book, *How Joyful People Think,*[45] Jamie Rasmussen, devotes the entire book to one verse of scripture taken from the book of Philippians. That one verse lists eight virtues, "Whatever is true, whatever is noble, whatever is right, whatever is pure, whatever is lovely, whatever is admirable – if anything is excellent or praiseworthy – think about such things."[46] By focusing on these eight things, our lives can be filled with joy.

Our thoughts bring us joy. Thinking on these things teaches us to think as God would think. Then we can be filled with his joy. There is so much negative around us today. To be filled with joy, it is imperative that we make our focus on these eight things. When we focus on the negative, we grow negative, and we can lose our joy.

Conversely, when we focus on what is true, noble, right, pure, lovely, admirable, excellent, or praiseworthy, we become more joy filled. Do your own checkup. Are you becoming more or less filled with joy? If the answer is less joy, then change your focus and focus one by one on the criteria that Paul mentions.

[45] Rasmussen, Jamie, *How Joyful People Think,* Baker Books, 2018
[46] NIV, Philippians 4:8

Peace

"You, Lord, give perfect peace to those who keep their purpose firm and put their trust in you. "[47]
-Isaiah

As a mature woman, I would not classify myself as a peaceful person. I am constantly on the go and find it a challenge to sit. Encouraged by a pastor, several years ago, my husband, our pastor and his wife and a friend, and I made a pilgrimage to a small village in France called Taize.

I had many misgivings about spending a week in a place of peace. What would that be like? I feared having to sit still a lot because as you know, that is something I do not do. Being reflective is not in my DNA. I did not want to be reflective.

The community of Taize was founded in 1940, by a man named Brother Roger who was 25 years old at the time of its founding. Brother Roger fled Switzerland where World War II was raging to this small village in the south of France. Brother Roger was motivated by the example of his maternal grandmother to help others find refuge. She set the example by allowing people to stay in her home near Paris. Taizé was begun to welcome refugees who were trying to go south.

---

[47] American Bible Society, *The Holy Bible*, Isaiah 26:3, Today's English Version, 1992, p. 630

During WWII, the community was forced to stop for about 2 years, but they were able to resume again. Brother Roger wanted to establish a community where people could live out their faith. His goal was to create a place where the goodness of heart and simplicity would be the center of everything.

Today, people from all over the world visit Taize. There are over 100 brothers of both Catholics and Protestant faiths.[48] When you visit Taize you will find worship that is contemplative and meditative. It is mostly attended by young people from all over the world, but 5 of us not so young went there to spend a week to learn, study, and be refreshed.

During the week that you are there, time is spent in community prayer in a meaningful service of worship three times a day. Moreover, there is small group sharing, and discussion and reflection. The accommodations are amazingly simple and sparse. You bring your own linens.

---

[48] *Taize, Opening Paths of Trust,* Le Presses of Taize

Housekeeping and food preparation are done by the people attending. The worship services are very elegantly but simply adorned with many candles. Worshippers sit on the floor, and the brothers kneel for the entire service. The singing is in many languages, but mostly French.

I do not speak any French at all, but the music is so beautiful that it is not necessary to have a literal translation. The brothers call it free flow worship, and a brother lets the spirit lead him as to how long a song should be. There is only a French horn for accompaniment and the singing is done as a chant. The only words that are spoken and not sung are the reading of scripture in at least 3 languages.

Throughout the week, I could feel the peace that permeated the place. People from many lands, most of them much younger than us, and they were speaking many languages. Moreover, we all felt the oneness of being in the Lord's presence. There was a sense of reverence that permeated the entire week.

Despite my misgivings, I was able for one week to find the peace that usually evades me. As I was preparing to write this chapter, I went back to the journal that I wrote during that week at Taizé and relived a bit of that peaceful time with the Lord. I rediscovered that when I listen to the music from Taizé I am able to recapture a bit of that peace.

As I look back at that time, I am able to remember what helped me then. For me, finding that peace will always be a struggle, but one I know that only with God's help, I can find the peace. What is it for you? What brings you peace? Pray about that, and if this is something with which you, like me, struggle, ask the Lord to reveal to you what it is that gives you peace.

Patience

"Everyone feels benevolent if nothing happens to be annoying him at the moment."
-C. S Lewis

The Bible is rife with admonitions about avoiding anger, but little is said about how one should go about doing that. In the Bible, there are nine references to the Lord being slow to anger. These include some form of the words "abounding in love." It would be safe to assume that a person with patience would be slow to anger and abounding in love.

Encyclopedia.com defines patience as "The quality or virtue of patience is presented as either forbearance or endurance. In the former sense, it is a quality of self-restraint or of not giving way to anger, even in the face of provocation. In the latter sense, it is a virtue by which one bears the trials of this life with resignation to God's will."

With regard to forbearance, there are two aspects, God's patience with us and our learning to be patient with others. First, there is no better example than God's patience with humankind. Over and over in the Bible, we see people disobey, and we see God being patient with that disobedience. Of course, after much patience, he decides a punishment is in order. That is not due to a lack of love, or even a lack of patience, but sometimes the only way learning can take place is through punishment.

In reflecting about the Israelites wandering through the desert for 40 years, I previously focused on how difficult that must have been on those people. In working through thoughts on God's patience, I realized just how patient God was with them. Over and over, he gave them clear directions. Over and over, they disobeyed.

Throughout the history of Israel, many kings ruled. Some were good and others were evil. Some tried to follow God's precepts, and others were blatant in their refusal to adhere to those precepts. I am always amazed when I read about the history of the kings in the Bible, and it ends with the statement that a particular king did evil in the eyes of the Lord. Eventually, after repeated disobedience, the Lord allowed Israel to fall into captivity.

We see the same patience reflected in the life of Jesus. His disciples did not understand his mission. He taught them anyway. Society at the time misunderstood him. He loved, healed, and ministered to them anyway. He was falsely accused. He bore that and never even uttered a word in his own defense. He died a painful death on a cross to bear our sin. His life was lived in patience with mankind.

Personally, I am eternally grateful, that he has been and continues to be patient with me. I basically left my faith when I was 20 and did not return until I was 44.

He did not say, "I quit. This is taking too long for Jackie to return to her faith." He hung with me until I was ready to return. Truly he has been faithful to me and faithful with me.

Since God is so patient with us, it is only right that we must learn to be patient with others. Patience comes in many forms. We live in a highly stressed world. According to the American Institute of Stress, over 70% of Americans regularly experience physical and psychological symptoms caused by stress.[49] In attempting to fill many roles as spouses, parents, caregivers, employees, bosses, etc. there are often not enough hours in the day.

---

[49] https://www.stress.org/daily-life

When I got my master's degree almost 50 years ago in Health, Physical education, and Recreation, it was predicted that within 20 years, Americans would have a greatly reduced workweek and much more time for leisure activities. It was predicted that we would eventually have a thirty-hour workweek. The prediction was that people would have more time for recreation. That simply has not materialized. In an article for *The Nation*, Bryce Covert stated, " Nearly a third of American employees clock 45 or more hours at work each week, and about 10 million put in 60 hours or more. Americans of prime working-age now work 7.8 percent more hours than they did four decades ago." [50]

With work being a prime producer of stress, we must realize that much of our population is experiencing some degree of stress. That means we must ask for patience in our dealings with others and pray that they are asking for patience in dealing with us.

Regarding the endurance aspect of patience, we need to learn to endure. Endure what? We need to endure whatever does not go the way we expect. We live in an age of instant gratification. Whatever it is that we want, we want it now. Entire industries have been built on getting people goods and services faster.

---

[50] https://www.thenation.com/article/archive/americans-work-too-much-already/

As people, we simply do not like to wait. Personally, it is something at which I have never excelled. Regretfully, I notice as I have gotten older, I am becoming even less patient. When I have to wait, I am grateful for an electronic device to keep me entertained while I wait. What did I do before electronic devices? Usually, books kept me entertained. I marvel at those who can just sit and wait patiently. That would certainly not be my strong suit. In the middle of writing this chapter, I went for a bike ride. I had to cross a busy intersection. The cross-traffic was non-stop. I was trying to cross that traffic, but there were no cars waiting to cross at the light where I was. Since I am not big enough on a bike to set off a traffic signal, I have to get off my bike and go to the crosswalk to push the button for the crosswalk.

I must admit I get a little annoyed at having to interrupt my ride. On this day, I waited through one set of cross-traffic light changes and then another. By the time, the third round of cross-traffic changes went, I was not happy. My patience with the traffic light was gone. Rather than continue to wait and maybe never see the light change, I just went another way. Then I thought, if I do not have any patience with the little things of life, how will I ever be patient with the bigger things?

Research tells us that we now have a shorter attention span than a goldfish with a goldfish having a nine-second attention span and we having an eight-second attention span.[51] What does that mean for us? It is certainly not contributing to our patience levels. As we use the Internet more and more, we demand faster web page openings. In an article for Digital Vault, Paul Dughi states, "How long will consumers wait for a page to load while shopping for your products? Turns out, not very long.

In a study of 4,500+ consumers, *Imperva Incapsula* reported that 7% say the page must load immediately or they are gone. 20% say less than 3 seconds of load time is acceptable. 35% said they'd wait between 3 and 5 seconds." [52]

All this is to show that, as a society, we are becoming less and less patient. Try as we might, we are not going to be able to become a more patient person and endure without the help of the Holy Spirit.

---

[51] https://time.com/3858309/attention-spans-goldfish
[52] https://medium.com/digital-vault/how-long-will-customers-wait-for-your-site-to-load-we-put-top-sites-to-the-test-545862be62c

Kindness

"Constant kindness can accomplish much. As the sun makes ice melt, kindness causes misunderstanding, mistrust, and hostility to evaporate." [53]
-Albert Schweitzer

Following along with the order in which the fruit of the spirit is listed by Paul, we see that kindness follows love and patience. This is not random. Kindness is a fruit of God's Spirit at work in us. Kindness is not something that comes naturally to many of us. Our general tendency is me first, and then others.

To practice kindness, one first must be full of love. Being full of love, patience with others follows. Because we are full of God's love and patience, then it becomes possible to practice kindness. What then is kindness? Very simply put, kindness is caring for others above yourself. The *NIV Bible* lists 56 references to the word kindness with surprisingly 45 of them in the Old Testament and eleven in the New Testament.

Several acts of kindness began the lineage of Jesus as told in the story of Ruth from the Old Testament. That story begins with Naomi a Moabite, who was married to an Israelite named Elimelech.

---

[53] https://www.brainyquote.com/quotes/albert_schweitzer_121165

They had two sons and lived in Israel. When there was a famine in Israel, they moved to the country of Moab. The sons married Moabite women, Ruth and Orpah. Elimelech died in Moab, and after some time the sons also died.

In those times, widows without male heirs were unprotected and not cared for. Naomi heard that the Lord was blessing Israel by giving them good crops. She made plans to go there to find her husband's kin. Despite Naomi's protests, Ruth went with her. That was truly kind of Ruth.

Once in Bethlehem, Ruth went to the fields of a wealthy relative of her father-in-law, Boaz, and asked to be able to glean the fields. Boaz was impressed by Ruth's loyalty to Naomi, and he was kind to her. She was given permission to glean Boaz's fields plus the assurance that she would not be molested. They still needed to find a husband for Ruth, and Naomi instructed her to go and sleep at Boaz's feet.

When Boaz woke up and found Ruth, she asked him to marry her. Rather than rebuking her for this brash action, Boaz blessed her. He said "The Lord bless you. "You are showing me even greater family loyalty in what you are doing now than in what you did for your mother-in-law. You might have gone looking for a young man, either rich or poor, but you haven't."[54]

---

[54] Holy Bible, Today's English Version, Ruth 3:10

In marrying Ruth, Elimelech's property was able to stay in the family. Ruth and Boaz had a son. His name was Obed. Obed was the father of Jesse, and Jesse was the father of David. Throughout this story we see kindness after kindness. What story could be a better way to start the lineage of Jesus?

Throughout the New Testament, we see the many kindnesses of Jesus. He was always stopping what he was doing and healing someone. When he saw a need he responded with kindness and warmth. He often showed kindness to those who were rejected by the rest of society. This is very counterculture for us. Many times, what stops us from being kind is our focus on something else.

I will always have a fondness for Sydney, Australia. This is due to the kindness of a stranger toward my husband and me while we were touring there. First, it was formerly a British colony, so they still drive on the left side of the road. As a pedestrian, you must be mindful to watch out for traffic in a way that you are not accustomed. Rather than trying to move through the traffic above ground, we decided underground might be less stressful.

Armed with a map, we were trying to navigate underground to get to a particular place. With no landmarks, that was even more challenging in a strange place. We got very lost. A kind woman came along and asked if we were lost. We said we were. She asked where we were trying to go. We told her, and rather than just showing us on the map, she walked us several blocks out of her way underground to get us to where we needed to be.

When I think of kindness, her example always comes to mind. Practicing kindness is not easy, and it always costs us something. That could be time, money or even esteem. I am certain the lady in Sydney was going somewhere, but she stopped and helped strangers. Even though I remember her kind act, I believe she would not remember it specifically. I would imagine that being kind is just a part of her character. Christopher Wright says, "Kindness goes beyond duty – it means doing something that you don't have to do, but just choose to do. Kindness goes beyond reward.

In fact, real kindness usually costs something and does not expect any reward. You do kindness for its own sake and for the sake of the other person. In that sense kindness is its own reward."[55]

---

[55]https://www.crufoundation.org/christopher-j-h-wright-biblical-kindness/

Kindness is about being aware of people around us and how we might be able to serve them. It is about encouraging someone who is in a difficult situation or simply thanking someone who is serving us.

Remembering to be kind is something with which I personally struggle. I am the type of person who focuses on what I need to get done. Being interrupted is not something I enjoy. Even in my communication, I must constantly remind myself to start out with a nice greeting. I would rather just get on with the business of what I must do. It is great to know that since this is a challenge for me, I can get some help in the area just by praying for that and becoming more aware of being kind. Hopefully, I can become just a little kinder day by day. Through the writing of this chapter, I realize that I still have a long way to go.

Goodness

"Man has two spiritual needs; one is for forgiveness. The other is for goodness."
-Billy Graham[56]

While searching the Internet for stories about goodness, I was reminded of the goodness of a senior officer to this young Air Force wife many years ago. My husband, Dick, was new in the Air Force, and we were newlyweds. Dick had just become the copilot of an F4 phantom fighter jet, his dream job. He had to go through training. The pilot, Colonel Rice, had come to the same training with my husband. The training was only about nine months, so he had come without his family. I invited him to join us for dinner. Previously, Colonel Rice had been an aide to a very high-ranking general officer, and I was intimidated.

Cooking was a new experience for me, and I lacked confidence about entertaining. I found out he liked lemon meringue pie and hesitantly made one. I had never even attempted one before. When I served it, he asked if I had made it and I nervously said I had.

---

[56] https://www.brainyquote.com/quotes/billy_graham_385542?src=t_goodness

He complimented me and told me, "My wife would have never had the balls to do that when she was your age." Of course, I immediately liked him and relaxed.

The pie was not really all that great, but his goodness overwhelmed me. What he did to bolster this young insecure wife was immeasurable.

While Colonel Rice certainly did a good deed in affirming me, his goodness is not what is described as a fruit of the spirit. What is that goodness? Kelly Wise Valdez says," The Bible tells us that the word 'good' actually means holy, pure and righteousness.

Another definition of goodness is one that I read on a blog post on Ospreyobserver.com, which says goodness is godliness. That puts a whole new connotation on the word. Not only are we to be kind to others, but we must also do what is morally right according to God's standards. That is a tall order, but just like the other fruit of the Spirit, it can only be done when we seek the power that is only available through the Holy Spirit.

We do this by studying God's playbook, the Bible, and by acting out of true goodness of the heart. Goodness is an action, practiced over time. In a blog for Grand Canyon University, Lauren Abraham says, "When we act out of true goodness of the heart, we are obedient to God's commandments and seek the benefit of others. Our actions come from a place of selflessness, and we place the needs of others before our own."[57]

The prophet Daniel continually showed God's goodness. He did what was right in the sight of the Lord. He was an Israelite political administrator working as a captive in Babylonia, and in Persia at the end of his life. In all that he did he had a spirit of excellence.

As with many who exhibit excellence in all that they do, sometimes others resent this excellence. Knowing that Daniel would never give up his worship of God, those who resented him, devised a plan to make Daniel choose between worshipping God or bowing down to the king. Despite the threat of death, Daniel chose to remain faithful to God. Through all he did Daniel manifested God's goodness. This is not to say that we are saved by our actions, but rather that we are saved so that we can do good works and show others the goodness of God.

---

[57] https://www.gcu.edu/blog/spiritual-life/weekly-devotional-fruit-spirit-goodness

The other example of goodness comes from modern times. This was given to me by my friend, Chris Van Matre. I asked my Facebook group *(An Upward Climb toward Faith)* for their thoughts on goodness. She sent me this quote from Geoff Pentz's Facebook page. I am quoting the whole post which referred to Nelson Mandela.

"After becoming President, I asked some of my bodyguard members to go for a walk. After the walk, we went for lunch at a restaurant. We sat in one of the most central ones, and each of us asked what we wanted. After a bit of waiting, the waiter who brought our menus appeared. At that moment I realized that at the table that was right in front of ours there was a single man waiting to be served. When he was served, I told one of my soldiers: go ask that man to join us. The soldier went and transmitted my invitation. The man stood up, took the plate and sat next to me. While eating, his hands were constantly shaking and he didn't lift his head from the food. When we finished, he waved at me without even looking at me, I shook his hand and walked away! The soldier said to me: - Madiba, that man must be very sick as his hands wouldn't stop shaking while he was eating. Not at all! The reason for his tremor is another, I replied. They looked at me weird and I said to them. That man was the guardian of the jail I was locked up in. Often, after the torture I was subjected to, I screamed and cried for water and he came to humiliate me, he laughed at me and instead of giving me water he urinated on my head. He wasn't sick, he was scared and shook, maybe fearing that I, now that I'm president of South Africa, would send him to jail and do the same thing he did with me, torturing and humiliating him. But that's not me, that behavior is not part of my character nor my ethics. Minds that seek revenge destroy states, while those that seek reconciliation build nations. " -Nelson Mandela[58]

Lastly, God's goodness is shown to us in his ultimate gift, his son, Jesus Christ. God gave his only son that we may be forgiven of all our sins. In Jesus, we have been set free from sin and death from that sin. We have been given new life. The apostle, John, quoting Jesus, says, "The thief comes to steal and kill and destroy; I have come that they may have life and have it to the full. I am the good shepherd. The good shepherd lays down his life for the sheep." [59] What could be a more perfect example of goodness?

[58] https://www.facebook.com/YodaDad/posts/10223651526052167
[59] *NIV*, John 10: 10, 11

Faithfulness

"For great is your love, reaching to the heavens; your faithfulness reaches to the skies."
The Psalms[60]

In a sermon, Ricky Jenkins, of Southwest Church, Coachella Valley, tied faithfulness to integrity. The word integrity evolved from the Latin adjective integer meaning whole or complete. Wikipedia defines faithfulness as "in this context, integrity is the inner sense of wholeness deriving from qualities such as honesty, and consistency of character."

In other words, integrity is who you are when no one else is watching. The person who stays true to his or her faith no matter the situation has the integrity of faith and can be called faithful. A person who has high faith integrity remains the same in public or in private.

How then does one develop faithfulness? In my grandson's Taekwondo class, the master is always stressing to the children, "Do the right thing at the right time."[61] That is a simple explanation of integrity. Faithfulness hinges upon what we value as important combined with our commitment of staying true to that.

---

[60] *NIV*, Proverbs 18:8
[61] Mascolina, Jeff, Kicks Taekwando, Riverside, CA

Why is it such a challenge to do the right thing at the right time? We are not so different from those kids in my grandson's class. We just have created more excuses along the way to convince ourselves that we are only doing what needs to be done at the time.

Faithfulness comes from a place of trust and loyalty. This is what we need in all our relationships, marriage, friends, and our relationship with the Lord. God never breaks his promises, but it is not so with people. Hebrews 11:1 says, "Now faith is confidence in what we hope for and assurance about what we do not see."[62]

---

[62] *NIV*, Hebrews 11:1

Many lessons can be learned from the Biblical story about Abraham. His story is told in the book of Genesis.[63] He was called Abram, at the time. He was 75 years old and living in a place called Haran far away from what is now Israel. He was a man of faith. God told him to leave his home and travel to the land of Canaan. This was no small journey and required a lot of faith to break up his home, leave his friends, and travel with his family and a lot of livestock many miles through unfamiliar lands. All he had was God's promise that God would make a great nation from him. He had no children at the time and a wife who was apparently barren.

However, he acted in faith and made that long journey. There were several missteps along the way. His wife, who eventually was named Sarah by God, became impatient on not bearing a child. She gave her handmaiden to Abraham to produce an offspring. That act led to all sorts of problems. While visiting Israel, our tour guide, David, continually used the Hebrew word "balagan" to describe situations like this. We can best translate it to "a mess." Abraham had many "balagans" occurring in his life, but, despite it all, he remained faithful.

---

[63] *NIV,* Genesis 12: 1 - 25:11

To continue the story, Sarah, finally stopped trying to take matters in her own hands and acted in faith toward God's promises. Even though she was past childbearing years, she was able to conceive, and a son was born. Those steps of faithfulness led to the founding of the nation of Israel. Taking that first step across the desert must have been daunting. It is a challenge for me to even imagine that kind of faith.

On that same trip to the Holy Land, we took a short camel ride out into the Judean desert. I was awed at the nothingness of the Judean desert. Even though Israel is a small country, all I could see was nothing but sand for many miles. The camel ride I took was far from comfortable, but short in duration.

My mind went back to Abraham all those years ago setting out on a promise from God. What tremendous faith that must have taken! I am certain he must have faced many doubts, but he persisted and became the father of a nation. HIs story continues through thirteen chapters in the book of Genesis. Throughout it all, we see that Abraham was not a perfect man, but he was faithful. There were many more times that he had to act out of faith, and by and large, he did.

We might be tempted to say that was years ago, and God doesn't make those kinds of promises today. I believe that the Word of God is unchangeable, and he did say he would never forsake us. The book of Joshua says, "Never will I leave you; never will I forsake you."[64] He doesn't leave us. We leave Him. That can be conscious (like I did so many years ago) or unconscious when we just get too busy to plug into God through prayer or his word through scriptures. Being faithful is an ongoing process.

In the story about Abraham, the person whom the Bible portrays as a man of great faith, we see a lot of Abraham stumbling. That frees us up to know that becoming a faithful person is an ongoing process. It is exceedingly difficult for us, but through the help of the Holy Spirit, it becomes never easy, but doable.

---

[64] *NIV*, Joshua 1:5b

As we close this chapter, I want you to ask, "Am I a faithful person?" Is this an area where you struggle? Are there things getting in the way of your faithfulness? If so, what are they? Ask God to help you to become more faithful.

Gentleness

"Don't do anything from selfish ambition, or from a cheap desire to boast, but be humble toward one another, always considering others better than yourself."
– Apostle Paul[65]

Some translations of the Bible list this fruit as humility rather than gentleness. That gives a broader word picture of what this could mean. Whichever word you choose, these have not always been virtues valued in society. As a matter of fact, through the years, they have been looked down upon as being unmanly. Unfortunately, that is not much different today. Today's superhero man still permeates much of our media. Let us explore two questions. 1) What does gentleness as a fruit of the spirit mean? 2) Why is gentleness important for us today?

In a weekly devotional, Lauren Abraham states, "A common misconception is that gentleness is weakness or passivity. True gentleness, however, is just the opposite. It requires great strength and self-control. Gentleness comes from a state of humility."[66]

---

[65] TEV, Philippians 2:3b

[66] Abraham, Lauren, *Weekly Devotion-Fruit of the Spirit,* https:www.gcu.edublog, January 22, 2016

In thinking through this chapter, I asked the members of the Facebook Group created for this book what gentleness meant to them and why was it important in our world today. I love the one I got from Debbie Johnson, "The best answer I have seen for gentleness is self-forgetfulness."[67] Another great definition of gentleness comes from Trask and Goodall saying, "Gentleness is strength under control."[68]

These should eliminate all thoughts that the characteristic of gentleness is a wimpy kind of thing. Rather it is powerful. When others lash out at us, we can stay calm and in control of the situation. True gentleness requires self-control which is the subject of the next chapter.

We see many examples of both God and Jesus being gentle in the Bible. God is often referred to as a shepherd, one who guards and cares for his flock. Formerly, we lived near fields where sheep could roam free. You could watch the shepherds tenderly tending to their flock. Jesus, too, shows many examples of gentleness.

My favorite is when he not only forgave Peter for denying him but reinstated him. Jesus must have been extremely disappointed, but he chose a gentle route.

---

[67] Johnson, Debbie, Facebook Group for *An Upward Climb toward Faith* Book

[68] Trask, Thomas and Goodall, Wayde, *The fruit of the Spirit,* Nashville, TN, Emanate Books, 2000, p. 136

Gentleness continues to be important for us today. We live in a world of chaos and the media feeds that frenzy. Media today does not promote behaving with a gentle spirit.

Over thirty years ago I was challenged by a book I read, called *See You at the Top.*"[69] In that book, the author challenged readers to go on a TV diet and not watch TV for a year.

It seemed impossible, but I decided to do it. To this day, I do not watch network TV. I count that as a contributor toward my positive attitude. We are indeed affected by what we watch. How can I grow in gentleness when I am being bombarded by watching behaviors, words, and deeds that are unkind? That takes us to social media.

Social media should reflect the person that you would like to become. Due to controversial posts, many people are giving up social media. With a heated election and a pandemic, the year 2020 was a year of year of controversy. There were many poisonous posts and people were saying things that they would never say face to face. It became a challenge to not respond and just let these angry posts go.

To become gentler, we need to practice mercy and give others the grace that we would like to have for ourselves. The words that come to mind is being tenderhearted. We are all human and make mistakes. When someone makes a mistake or says something in anger, we need to be the bigger person

---

[69] Ziglar, Zig, *See You at the Top,* Pelican Publishing, 1982

and just let it go. By blasting one another, are we making the situation better or worse? Practicing gentleness is not easy. It takes a lot of forethought, self-control, and practice.

The adage of "Count to ten before you speak," verbally or on social media gives much wisdom.

Self-Control

"For the Spirit God gave us does not make us timid, instead, his spirit fills us with power, love and self-control."[70]
— Apostle Paul

What a compelling statement this is that Spirit fills us with power, love, and self-control. Who would not love to have these attributes? To conclude this section on the Fruit of the Spirit, the last fruit should be taken as the culmination of the other eight. Drew Dyck states, "Self-control isn't just one good character trait, a nice addition to the pantheon of virtues, it's foundational. Not because it is more important than other virtues, but because the others rely upon it." [71]

All the other qualities are virtues that God himself possesses, but the last, self-control, is not something God needs. God is already perfect, sinless, and without any need of self-control. We are neither perfect nor sinless, and we are much in need of self-control. What is self-control? Dyck defines it as "the ability to do the right thing even when you do not feel like it."[72]

---

[70]*TEV*, 2 Timothy 1:7
[71] Dyck, Drew, *Your Future Self Will Thank you, Secrets to Self-Control from the Bible and Brain Science,"* Chicago: Moody Publishers, 2019, p.13
[72] IBID, p. 33

It is easy to spot the lack of self-control in a life, but much more difficult to understand how to develop it. When a person has little self-control, someone else will control them and their freedom will be lost. An example would be a person suffering from an addiction. The addiction controls them. Another example would be a person who has gone to prison for a crime. Then they are controlled by the prison.

Self-control without the Spirit is almost impossible. As we become more Christlike, the Fruit of the Spirit becomes more evident in our lives, but we must be constantly on guard to edify God and follow his precepts. This is not something that we can do on our own, but self-control is given to us by God when we spend time with him.

Let me be perfectly clear here. God gives us his grace when we say that Jesus is our savior. There is nothing we can do to earn this. It is a gift pure and simple. However, when we spend time with him, we can become more Christlike by exercising control over those things which are not Christlike. We do this in three practical ways: 1) by reading God's word daily, 2) by praying for help with what we struggle, and 3) by having mentors and being accountable. Each of these is discussed in other chapters.

You might ask, how does Godly self-control differ from willpower? The difference is who is in charge. Dyck defines willpower as "the emotional energy needed to withstand temptation. It's the fuel that enables self-control.[73]

Here's the rub, though. We have a limited amount of willpower. In a famous experiment, college students were challenged with eating radishes and resisting chocolate chip cookies. Resisting the chocolate chip cookies drained the willpower of the participants and they were challenged in trying next to solve a difficult puzzle. Since they had resisted the chocolate chip cookies, it was more difficult for them to persist in solving the puzzle. Ray Baumeister and his team concluded that willpower is limited. They called this ego depletion.[74] When we use willpower to do or not do something, we are in control of the process, but our willpower can only carry us only so far. That is why groups like Alcoholics Anonymous (AA) have been so successful. First, they acknowledge a higher power. They realize that people cannot make it on their own. They admit that they cannot control it themselves. Their willpower just is not enough.

Then, they become a part of a community of people all trying to do the same thing. When we exhibit Godly self-control, God is working through us in the process. Godly self-control is the ability to submit our will to the will of God. In self-control, we become willing to make the changes that God wants for us. Sometimes this is a conscious process; other times it is not.

---

[73] *Ibid*, p.78

[74] Baumeister, Roy et al, "Ego Depletion. Is the Active Self a Limited Resource?" *Journal of Personality and social Psychology 74, No. 5,* 1998, p. 1254

The hand gesture in sign language for self-control is like steering the bridle of a horse with the hands making a steering motion. We have a choice to go our way or God's way. A great example of self-control was Jesus in the Garden of Gethsemane on the night that he was arrested.

He was so grieved at what he was supposed to do that he sweat blood. Three times he prayed and asked if it was possible that he not have to go through with what God had planned. He also prayed each time that if this was not possible, God's will be done. He was able to submit his will to the will of his father. This was the ultimate in self-control.[75] We seem to live in an out of control, short-tempered society.

One aspect of this is a phenomenon called road rage. That is when a driver exhibits violent behavior because of frustration from driving in difficult situations. There has been an increase in road rage in the past twenty years.

An article on Fox News states, "Fatalities resulting from crashes linked to aggressive driving increased from 80 instances in 2006 to 467 in 2015 — that's almost a 500 percent increase in just ten years." [76] What are some reasons for this? It is not just more drivers on the road, but less patience and self-control on the part of drivers.

---

[75] *TEV*, Matthew 26:39 - 44
[76] https://www.fox5dc.com/news/road-rage-fatalities-increased-500-percent-over-10-years-and-theyre-still-on-the-rise-study-says

I have a wonderful friend who formerly had little patience and was an overly aggressive driver. He jokingly called his numerous tickets "driving awards." When he was being reckless, he said that Bob (not his name) was in control. Now he is a careful driver. I asked him, "What changed?" He told me that first he asked Jesus into his life and committed his life to him. Then he started listening to nothing but Christian music. Little by little through that music, the Holy Spirit changed his life. By following the promptings of the Holy Spirit, he was able to change. No discussion on self-control would be complete without a bit of time devoted to screen and social media. Experts do not agree on the number of hours, but it is safe to say that the average is four to six hours per day on video and 11 or so hours all together on media. Nielson reported, "According to the firm's research, U.S. adults are now spending almost 6 hours per day on video, on average.

That includes time spent watching both live and time-shifted TV, watching videos in an app or mobile website on a smartphone or tablet, watching video over a TV-connected device like a DVD player, game console or internet device such as Roku, and watching videos on a computer. That data on video viewing was collected during the first quarter of 2018 – and accounts for a sizable chunk of the 11 hours per day Americans spend listening to, watching, reading, or otherwise interacting with media." [77]

With many people stuck in their homes during the pandemic of 2020. I suspect that number would be higher. Of course, in 2020, much screen time was spent in either online schooling or working from home, so it would be difficult to get accurate results in 2020. The article above goes on to say, "Beyond video, Nielsen's report also examines social media adoption. It found adults are spending an average of 45 minutes per day on social media, with most of that time on smartphones." So, what do these statistics mean?

There are more and more places for us to exercise self-control. You may wonder, "What is the harm?" The harm is our minds are being deadened by all these distractions.

Think of all the ploys to get us to behave in a certain way, buy a certain product, or look at subjects that would not normally be easily accessible to us.

Talk about temptations! I recently saw a post on social media that made me angry. The person posted some very slanderous political cartoons. It is fine to give your viewpoints, but slander is never acceptable.

Of course, I was of the opposite political view. I do not think she would have said what she said in person. With social media, the gloves seem to be off for some people. I guard what I post and only post about my God, my family or positive things.

---

[77] https://techcrunch.com/2018/07/31/u-s-adults-now-spend-nearly-6-hours-per-day-watching-video/

I must admit though, the first thing that went through my mind was to give her a piece of mine. I did that once and the results were disastrous. I just quietly "unfriended" her. I did not want to give her the ability to anger me.

So, what about Facebook? The scary thing is that Facebook is designed to keep you there. The same is true of all the social media platforms, but we will focus on Facebook. When someone "likes" what you post, it gives you a little emotional boost, and you want more. You can become dependent upon that perceived social value. What the makers of Facebook want you to do is to stay there long enough that you will see the ads.

In an article for the Washington Post former Facebook executive, Chamath Palihapitiya, says, "It literally is at a point now where I think we have created tools that are ripping apart the social fabric of how society works.

That is truly where we are," he said. "The short-term, dopamine-driven feedback loops that we have created are destroying how society works: no civil discourse, no cooperation, misinformation, mistruth."[78] That man eventually left his Facebook position saying he could no longer be a part of it, and he forbade his children from using it.

---

[78] https://www.washingtonpost.com/news/the-switch/wp/2017/12/12/former-facebook-vp-says-social-media-is-destroying-society-with-dopamine-driven-feedback-loops/

Yes, I do enjoy reading what my friends are doing and looking at their family pictures. I have seen great things come from posts on Facebook, lost pets found, updates on local events, prayer requests, etc. We just need to be diligent and stay vigilant for those things that take us away from the Lord. Just like anything else, if you realize that social media is a problem for you, that may mean going off social media. Ask yourself if the time you spend online is contributing to your faith walk.

As we close this section on the fruit of the Holy Spirit, what is it that you would like to change and where would you like to grow?

Is it the ability to love, become more joy filled, peaceful, patient, full of goodness, faithfulness, gentleness, or self-controlled? All of those are the fruit of the Holy Spirit. These are available to all, but you must seek them earnestly. They do not come just because you ask. You must also seek and work at developing them. **We always have a choice to go our way or God's way. This is called free will.**

Remember, the famous theologian John Stott prayed earnestly and daily for the receipt of them, and he also spent much time in study, prayer, and the Christian community.

Gifts

"It all belongs to God."[79]
-Tom Lance – Grove Community Church

After living in Germany for four years and witnessing our friend's great faith, we returned to the United States. Upon our return, we were determined to put some teeth into our commitment to be churchgoers, and we joined a United Methodist Church in Bossier City, Louisiana. In joining that church, we promised to faithfully participate in a local congregation through our prayers, presence, gifts, and service. That was over forty years ago, and even though we are no longer a part of that particular church, we are still trying our best to follow that pledge. So, what does all that mean? The prayers, presence, and service are self-evident and will be discussed further in other chapters, but what about participating with our gifts?

---

[79] https://thegrove.cc/media/god-with-us/remembering-the-past-impacts-the-future/

Gifts are not just material gifts, but also include your time, talents, and resources. Those are dealt with also in other chapters. This chapter will only deal with financial resources. Martin Luther is quoted as saying, "People go through three conversions: the conversion of their head, their heart, and their pocketbook.
Unfortunately, not all at the same time." This tongue in cheek quote bears some truth. Why is it so important that we give our financial resources to the work of the Lord?

The quote at the start of this chapter came from my pastor on a recent Sunday when my church was launching a huge campaign that asks members to give sacrificially, over and above the tithe of ten percent that we normally give. For the past six years, the members of our church have met the yearly campaign goals every year. Once we understand that "it all belongs to God" why wouldn't we want to give back? We seem to have no problem tipping 10 – 20 % at restaurants for good service. Why wouldn't we want to give back to the giver of all things?

There are many references to giving in the Bible in both testaments. Perhaps the most quoted is in Malachi, "Bring the whole tithe (tenth) into the storehouse that there may be food in my house." "Test me in this, says the Lord God Almighty, "and see if I will not throw open the floodgates of heaven and pour out so much blessing that there will not be enough to store it."[80]There are many references just like this. In the agrarian society of that time, most gifts to the Lord were a tenth of the harvest or of the livestock. Today what we can infer is that the Lord asks us to give one tenth of our financial resources.

So why is it important to give to God?

> 1. **To return his love** – God has given everything to us: life, wonderfully engineered bodies complete with the best computer system ever devised and especially his son, Jesus Christ. How can we ever repay that? We return his blessing when we give to others. Giving is a natural response to his love.

---

[80] NIV, Malachi 3:10

2. Because God tells us we should – There are numerous passages that talk about giving to God. King David declares God's ownership of everything, "The earth is the Lord's and everything in it, the world and all who live in it."[81] We are just here as stewards. We have the power whether to be faithful stewards or not.

3. Because there is need – There is much need everywhere today in our church, in our community, and our world. Find something about which you are passionate and give a bit of your financial resources to that. For over the past twenty years, we have supported the education of two third world boys, through World Vision. The current boys are from Malaysia and Guatemala. It is a small sum for us, but it makes a huge difference for these two boys. One of us cannot do that much, but when you combine our gifts with those of others, much can be done.

---

[81] Ibid, Psalm 24:1

4. Because giving brings pleasure to us –
Without giving, we would be very selfish. Giving
breaks us out of this selfishness. Giving also brings
us pleasure and gives us worth. You can find many
studies on the value of giving to the person who is
doing the giving. There is a sense of satisfaction in
knowing that we are contributing to the work of the
Lord. When we take our gifts to those who need
them, they break out in thanksgiving to God. How
good it feels to share even a small part of that!

5. **To glorify God** – In his book, *The Bride,*
Renewing Our Passion for the Church, Charles
Swindol states that our purpose in life is to glorify
God.[82] In his letter to the Corinthians, Paul talks
about generosity. He talks about God loving a
cheerful giver and that God will always bless our
gifts.

---

[82] Swindoll, Charles, *The Bride: Renewing Our Passion for the Church, Zondervan,*
1994

He further goes on to say, "You will be enriched in every way so that you can be generous, on every occasion, and through us your generosity will result in thanksgiving to God."[83] When we take our gifts to those who need them, they will break out in thanksgiving to God. Not only do we glorify God and cause others to glorify him, but we can also know that we are pulling our fair share with both the recipients of the gift and the Lord. Being faithful stewards, we can meet the savior in worship knowing we have done our part.

Lastly, let us talk about the tithe. Back to the passage in Malachi,[84] where we are directed to bring one-tenth of what we have into the storehouse. Tithing is not so much about giving your financial resources as it is showing faith that you can trust God with all that you have including your financial resources. I remember being challenged many years ago to begin tithing. It was a scary thought, and we knew that we could not do ten percent immediately.

[83] *NIV*, 2 Corinthians 11
[84] Ibid, Malachi, 3:10

Some of you may even be thinking, "That's fine for you, but you haven't seen my budget." I remember vividly being in that same place many years ago. The only way we could get to ten percent was to increase our giving each year by a certain per cent.

After some years, we got there, and have been there ever since. Just in case you are worried about not having enough, our accountant says that she has never met a tither with financial challenges. One of my favorite quotes comes from Billy Graham. He says, "You can't outgive God."[85] From personal knowledge I can tell you that once you trust God with your finances, it gives you an incredible peace of mind. You may also find that it gives you better financial discipline. For a control freak like me, tithing was a huge step, but once we began to tithe, we have never looked back.

---

[85] https://billygraham.org/devotion/we-cant-out-give-god/

Practice Mercy and Be Forgiving

"The Lord is good to all and his mercy is over all that he has made."

-The Psalms[86]

Jen Wilken defines mercy as, "not getting what we deserve." [87] One of the best examples of God's mercy to an individual is found in the famous story of David and Bathsheba in the book of Second Samuel.[88] King David spots a beautiful woman named Bathsheba bathing. He has her brought to him and they conceive a child. When this happens, Bathsheba' s husband, and one of David's warriors, is away at the battlefield. David invites this faithful warrior to come home to rest and see his beautiful wife. David's hope is that they will make love while her husband is visiting. Her faithful warrior refuses to come home from the front saying it is his duty to stay and fight with his men.

David then asks the husband's commander to place him in the front of the battle lines. The husband is killed. When the prophet Nathan confronts David with his sins, David confesses and repents. Not only has David committed adultery, but he perpetrated a murder. Either of those sins were punishable by death, but the Lord did not strike David down.

---

[86] *The Holy Bible, English Standard Version,* Psalm 145:9, Crossway, 2008
[87] Wilen, Jen, *In His Image*, Wheaton, IL: Crossway, 2018, p. 72
[88] *TEV,* 2 Samuel 11 & 12

He showed David mercy for his sins. The Lord forgave David, but he did punish him severely. (You will have to read those chapters to see what the punishment was.) This mercy shown to King David is no different from the mercy shown to each of us every day.

Paul tells us in the book of Romans, "everyone has sinned and is far away from God's saving presence. But by the free gift of God's grace all are put right with him through Jesus Christ who sets them free." [89] This could not be any clearer. **Everyone sins.** However, Paul goes on to say, "For the wages of sin is death, but the gift of God is eternal life in Jesus Christ our Lord."[90]

Eternal life is a free gift from God. As a gift, it does not need to be paid back. He has saved us because of his mercy not because of any righteous acts that we have done. Our only response is to accept the gift. In accepting the gift, however, we do accept some responsibility. As we have been shown mercy, it is up to us, in turn, to be merciful toward others. Jesus tells us in the Sermon on the Mount, "Blessed are the merciful, for they will be shown mercy."[91]Remembering this, we can "turn the other cheek" toward others. We all have bad days.

---

[89] *TEV,* Romans 3:23-24
[90] *NIV,* Romans 6:23
[91] *Ibid,* Matthew 5:7

Treating others with dignity and respect when they are being difficult is not easy, but when we think of God's great sacrifice for us, everything becomes a little less difficult. Being merciful toward others requires time, practice, and prayer.

We see many instances of God's mercy to individuals such as King David and also to nations in the Bible. We might be tempted to think that being merciful is easy for God, but how about us? How can we be merciful? There is a great story told on the Saddleback Church website.[92] There is a teen, Andy, who is full of energy and mischief. He and friends begin by throwing water balloons at passing cars. As the boys are able to drive, the games progress to throwing water balloons while driving. One night they do this, and it happened to hit the vehicle of an off-duty policeman who is out on a date. The policeman gives chase for forty minutes. Because Andy is driving very recklessly and almost hits a motorcycle, the policeman decides to stop the chase. The boys think they have gotten away with something.

The next week the policeman shows up in uniform at the school. The officer read Andy his rights and prepared to arrest him. However, just before arresting him the officer looked at Andy and said, "You know, you look like a good kid, and I believe you are good.

---

[92] https://saddleback.com/watch/stories/2018/07/06/Mercy-on-Repeat

I just think you are full of energy and mischief. I'm not going to press charges — but I am going to tell your dad."

Fast forward to Andy growing up and moving to Japan. He got jilted by a girl and began to question his life. The whole time his mother was forwarding him sermons from her church, Saddleback Community Church in California. He became a Christian. One day when he was listening to a sermon, there was a guest speaker. Guess who it was! Officer Dave. Andy connected the dots and decided God had a purpose for his life. He moved back to California with his wife.

Now he gives back to his church and community. He is a special education teacher and supervises Saturday detention for kids who have managed to get themselves kicked out of the classroom. He tries to help them to learn how to channel their energies in a productive way. He is showing mercy to kids just as he was shown mercy.

One simple act of mercy from a police officer had a ripple effect in the lives of many others. We may never know how an act of mercy will impact a life or as in the case of Officer Dave, many lives. A part of being merciful is also to be forgiving. There are many acts of cruelty and injustice inflicted upon innocent people. They are too numerous to mention.

No matter how difficult, the perpetrator must be forgiven. This is not to say that you must like them, but the forgiving is to benefit the person who has been wronged. Without forgiving, the wronged person is doomed to a life of anger. Such was the case of former NFL player, Kermit Alexander.

In his book,[93] he describes the horrific wrongful shooting of his mother, sister and two nephews by a gang member. His family was mistaken for another on whom a hit had been ordered and all those members of Alexander's family were shot to death. For many years, Alexander walked the streets of Los Angeles ready to avenge the deaths. He was consumed by his hatred of these teens who robbed him of his family. The killer was captured, and Alexander discovered that he had known the gang member previously as a troubled youth in a Pop Warner football league.

He had witnessed that the young man was disruptive and had anger issues. Realizing that he had done nothing to intervene when the gang member was a youth, he forgave the killer. However, Alexander was still an angry man and he blamed his own inaction for the death of four family members. He still had to forgive one more person, himself.

---

[93] Alexander, Kermit, Gerould, Alex, and Snipes, Jeff, *The Valley of the Shadow of Death: A Tale of Tragedy and Redemption*, Atria Books, September 2015.

He was dating a woman who was trying to adopt a boy from hurricane ravaged Haiti. He went with her and met the boy who would eventually become their son. They married and flew to Haiti to pick up their boy, Clifford. When they got there, four kids were there waving goodbye to Clifford. They were Clifford's siblings. The Alexanders ended up adopting the whole family.

Alexander and his wife devoted their lives to raising these five kids who otherwise would not have had a chance. In this way, Alexander felt that he could redeem his inaction toward the troubled youth from the Pop Warner league.

God gives mercy lovingly and he wants us to do the same. Jesus tells us, "Blessed are the merciful, for they will be shown mercy." [94] Mercy and forgiveness go hand in hand. One can give mercy to a perpetrator, but until there is forgiveness, there can be no healing for the one who has been wronged.

In the letter to the Colossians, Paul tells us, "Bear with each other and forgive one another if any of you has a grievance against someone. Forgive as the Lord forgave you."[95] Forgive not because they deserve it but because it is the only way that you can heal. You must release the hurt for your own well-being.

---

[94] *NIV,* Matthew 5:7
[95] *Ibid,* Colossians 3:13

Resentment gives the person whom you are resenting control of your heart. Is there someone to whom you need to give mercy and forgiveness? Are you holding onto resentment? If so, ask God for his help.

Prayer

*"Prayer is simply communicating with God.
There's nothing magical at all about Christian prayer;
it's a matter of fact."*
-Robert Wagner[96]

There is probably no area of my Christian life where I struggle more than with prayer. As I stated in the introduction, this is not a how-to book, but a revelation of the struggles that I actually face. This chapter is for the person who, like me, struggles with personal prayer.

The whole being still is something at which I have never excelled. Many years ago, a dear friend was leading a guided meditation, and we were told to imagine that we were floating on our backs in the middle of a lake staring up at a beautiful blue sky. I was fine for a few seconds, then I started to giggle because even in the meditation, I started doing the backstroke. I wish I could say that over the years that has changed, but it has not.

Then I read a book called *Come as You Are*[97] that changed my life.

---

[96] Wagner, Robert, *Christian Prayer for Dummies,* Print on Demand from Amazon
[97] Southard, Betty, and Littauer, Marita, *Come As You Are*, Bethany House, 1999.

In it, they suggest that God made you just as you are, and we need to worship according to the way we are made. Let me tell you I am not made to be still. Many of my friends have tried to teach me how to sit still and meditate quietly, but that just does not work for me. All it did was frustrate me and made me feel like I could never have a spiritual life. I am a hard-driving, competitive, control freak person with little ability to be still. I believe God made me that way for a reason.

I learned to talk to God while I was on the move. I can communicate best, walking along a beach, or on a pathway to almost anywhere. The key is I must keep physically moving. I got adept at prayer darts. Those are the quick prayers that you kind of throw at God. I still do those. A situation that needs prayer will pop into my mind and then I will toss it to God. This is hardly a prayer life that should be recommended, but it does fit with my personality style.

I did stumble over something that has been immensely helpful to me, breath prayer. We did a class at my church on how to develop a breath prayer. After a lot of stops and starts, I found one that works well for me. The idea is that it is something that can be said over and over, repeated like a mantra as you inhale and exhale. It should be short and meaningful to you.

When I remember to do it, it helps me get through stressful situations. I am a bit claustrophobic, especially when it comes to having MRI's. I have had two MRI's done in my lifetime. Both times, I used the breath prayer to get through them. Armed with my breath prayer, I managed to do them without a sedative. I developed mine in a class. If you are serious about learning about breath prayers, I would recommend investigating them and developing one of your own. The idea is to use a verb and noun that is meaningful to you.

Given my restlessness, mine is, "Let your peace radiate in me." I think you understand the peace, but the verb radiate came from a time when sitting by the sea early in the morning, I was blessed by the radiance of the ocean.

I can still visualize the sparkle of the water shining up at me like a million diamonds. Just thinking about that can take me back to that peaceful time. I feel the radiance of the sun on the sea and the peace I felt that morning. There are many books on the topic.

One is *The Breath of Life Workbook – A Simple Way to Pray: A daily Workbook for Use in Groups.* [98] If you want to try some that others have done, there is a great article on the Internet by Bob Hosteler, *10 Breath Prayers.* [99] When you can't stop in a church or kneel, these short, simple prayers can be spoken in a single breath.

Even though my private prayer life leaves something to be desired, I have no challenges praying with others either individually or in a group. Many years ago, I read a book that I can neither remember the title nor the author. In it the author challenged his readers to never say, "I will pray for you," when you hear other's needs.

---

[98] Delbene, Ron, *The Breath of Life Workbook – A Simple Way to Pray: A daily Workbook for Use in Groups*
[99] https://www.guideposts.org/faith-and-prayer/prayer-stories/pray-effectively/10-breath-prayers

Rather than praying later, you should ask if you could pray with them right on the spot. I usually say, "I believe that the Lord wants me to pray for you right now. Would that be Ok with you?" I have only been refused twice. It always provides both the person for whom I am praying and me with a blessing.

Often it brings tears to the person for whom I am praying. When people are hurting, it is so appreciated. I never will forget my first prayer with a complete stranger. I was at the food court in a mall.

Armed with my new information on praying for others, I got into a conversation with a Korean lady. At that time, I was actively building an Amway business. I met people everywhere I went, looking for people who might be interested in that business.

I cannot begin to tell you how many times God has led me to start a conversation only to find that person has needed prayer. This particular lady had just lost her husband, and she was dealing with that loss. I have no idea what I prayed, but she was very encouraged by it. Those rather halting first steps have led me to pray for countless people whom I have met. Now, I am not apprehensive at all to pray when I sense a need.

My prayers are not full of flowery phrases, just a heartfelt statement for the needs of the person for whom I am praying. I know the Lord will lead me. I just must open my mouth. I am also able to give all the credit to God because I know that he has led me to them. I will often say, "God just wanted to let you know he cares about your situation (I actually name the situation).

He may not be able to communicate with you verbally but wanted you to know that he is listening and cares about you. He sent me to tell you that." I am going to give you that same challenge that I took so many years ago. When you hear a need, take a deep breath, and ask if you might pray for that person. Do not worry about what to say. Send out a quick prayer dart for help and know that he has got you covered. Pray and get ready to be blessed. The first time will only happen once and I promise, it is not painful. To get better, you just need to do it more often.

To start and just get your juices flowing, use this technique the next time you see a person asking for prayers on social media. Rather than popping in the prayer emoji or saying, "I'll pray for you," take a minute and make someone's day by putting a prayer on social media. Then they know that you have really prayed for them. You also profess your faith to anyone else who might be reading that post. Who knows what God can do with that?

As for me, I know that I have a lot of growth to go in my personal prayer life.

Presence

"There is a brotherhood within the body of believers, and the Lord Jesus Christ is the common denominator. Friendship and fellowship are the legal tender among believers."
J. Vernon McGee [100]

Have you ever heard anyone say, "I don't need to go to church; I can worship God just fine on my own." While that is absolutely true, it is so easy to make excuses about not spending time with the Lord.

Going to church keeps me grounded. Plus, we were designed to live in community. When I hear people talking about how they worship fine on their own, I always give the analogy of the campfire. It burns more brightly when it has many logs.

Once you start pulling logs out, the fire lessens and eventually will go out. To keep our faith burning brightly, we need to be immersed in our faith through regular church attendance and participation in smaller groups with others. The book of Acts is full of references to living in Christian community. It is no wonder that with all these little fires, the early church spread like wildfire despite unfathomable obstacles.

---

[100] https://www.whatchristianswanttoknow.com/christian-fellowshi-quotes-22-edifying-quotes/

We are told in Acts, "As a result, the Lord added to their number daily those who were being saved" [101]

As noted in the chapter on "Gifts," those wishing to join the United Methodist Church pledge to give their prayers, presence, services, and gifts. The founder of that denomination, John Wesley, thought that Christian community was so important, he dedicated much time to organizing what that should look like. He called it Christian Conference.

Basically, it divided people into voluntary subgroups who met together weekly for prayer, encouragement, and nurturing. It was not the objective of these to replace the larger church, but to enhance it and provide an opportunity for members to have a fuller Christian experience and to grow in their faith.

Wesley was concerned about declining membership in the church, and he devised this to help people to stay faithful. We would liken these today to the small groups found as a part of the culture of many churches.

They go by different names—small groups, cell groups, care groups, discipleship groups, grace groups, and breakout groups. Whatever they are called, the basic idea is the same: a small gathering of people interested in spiritual growth.

---

[101] *NIV,* Acts 2:46 – 47

Currently, my husband and I belong to a church that emphasizes small groups. We belong to one together for both genders. We also belong to one which is at the conclusion of men's or women's bible study and gender specific.

The ones of which we are a part are broad based in terms of age, occupation, and interests.

Close relationships can be formed when the members are willing to be real with one another. We have people who pray for us, support us, encourage us, and serve alongside us. We have people to whom we can minister or people who will minister to us.

It is much easier to address the needs of others in a small group. There is also a certain degree of accountability. Studying the Bible with others and discussing it gives different perspectives. Many times, I learn more from other believers than when I read the scriptures by myself. I enjoy both groups, the mixed gender and the women only. In groups of the same gender, it may be easier to share difficult topics. In mixed gender groups, you get a broader viewpoint.

I grew up and married in a small Presbyterian church in Ohio. Then I went through my "no time for God" phase and did not attend church for thirteen years. When I finally returned to church attendance, it was first to an Air Force non-denominational church and then to a small United Methodist church after we moved to Louisiana. We were happy in that church, but the Air Force moved us to California.

We became part of a United Methodist church which was forming. We were actively involved in that church and loved it. We belonged to that church for almost 30 years. Then our needs changed, and with much prayer and deliberation, we reached the difficult decision that it was time to change churches.

Because we loved the members of that community, it was an agonizing decision, but one that we needed.

Now, we are part of a large community church. Since this church is so large, we had to do things to get to know people. We got involved right away with things that interested us. Once we knew a few people, the church did not seem so large. If you do attend a large church, it is imperative that you find some ways to interact with people in smaller groups.

Whatever you choose, it is important to become part of a worshipping community. A good church fit is like being part of a family. Find a place where you can grow and then dive in. The more involved you become, the more you will find that your faith can grow through fellowship with others.

Churches are criticized because the expectation is that they should be perfect. That, however, is not a fair assumption. Churches are composed of people who are far from perfect and there are issues with people just like in every walk of life. Messy situations happen. A church should not be expected to be a factory for saints, but rather a hospital for sinners.

Rest

*Rest time is not wasted time. It is an economy to gather fresh strength... It is wisdom to take occasional furlough. In the **long run, we shall do more by sometimes doing less.**[102]*

- Charles Spurgeon

How important to God is rest? Bible Gateway lists 508 references to verses that contain the word, "rest" in some form or another. Thousands of years ago, after the creation of the world, we are told that God rested.

As a part of the law in the Old Testament, God commanded that we rest saying, "'There are six days when you may work, but the seventh day is a day of sabbath rest, a day of sacred assembly. You are not to do any work; wherever you live, it is a sabbath to the LORD." [103] The command is clear. It is easy to say but challenging to do.

As I think you have guessed by now, resting is something with which I really struggle. I have a difficult time implementing the above quote that begins this chapter but wish that I could. Busyness appears to be a modern illness from which I am not the only one to suffer. I once read that an acronym for busy is **B**eing **U**nder **S**atan's **Y**oke.

---

[102] https://www.christianquotes.info/quotes-by-topic/quotes-about-rest/
[103] *Niv,* Leviticus 23:3

When we do not take the time to rest in the Lord, we are much more apt to not hear and therefore follow guidance from the Holy Spirit. Since resting is not one of my best skills, and that is an understatement, I asked, again for help from my Facebook group. There were many great suggestions. Listing them in no particular order, members of the group wrote things like "being in nature, viewing sunrises or sunsets, time alone, sitting on a porch or in a swing, keeping a prayer journal, gardening, meditation, focusing on God's word, and the one I love best, holding a sleeping baby in your arms." I just saw one of those "remembering when" posts on Facebook that showed me with my grandson who was very tiny peacefully sleeping on my chest. Just seeing that picture gave me a moment of fond rest. I am sure there are many more, but the main theme is the popular saying, "Let go and let God!"

In the Facebook group for this book, Ellen Croswell Morrison gave a great insight. She said, "I am learning that if I allow myself to fully rest my physical body, I am better at demonstrating the fruit of the spirit (patience, kindness, self-control). If my physical body is tired, I am likely to be grumpy, impatient, and/or quick to object."

In an article for Lifeway, Phillip Nation said, "Resting in the Lord is a spiritual discipline. If all you do is take a nap; it is not a bad thing. But press further into this act. Rest as a spiritual act in which you say that you trust God beyond what you can accomplish for yourself.

It requires discipline on your part to stop your mind from spinning on about what needs to be done next. In resting, focus on God and your relationships rather than on your task list." [104] Any discipline takes time to master. However, it is like running a race. With running a race, you start small and gradually build up to the distance you eventually want. Learning to rest is the same. Begin small to rest in the Lord. Gradually, you can work your way up to where you would like to be.

If you, like me, have a challenge with taking a Sabbath, here is a suggestion that I got from my pastor, Tom Lance, in a sermon. He suggested that you begin with an hour or two on a specific day and just keep adding time. That seemed to me like a logical way to take a sabbath. The best part of this is that it is your sabbath, so you can make up the rules. Of course, you want to do the rules in conjunction with the Holy Spirit. The Spirit will notify you through your conscience if you are off base. Here is what I am doing.

I chose Sundays, and now I am able to rest until 4:00 PM. Here are my rules. No electronics except for my daily Bible App. On other days, I listen to a lot of books on my IPhone, so I do not allow that on my sabbath. I also avoid recreational shopping.

---

[104] https://www.lifeway.com/en/articles/how-to-rest-in-the-lord

If I need to run to the grocery store, that is OK, but major shopping trips are confined to other days. I attend church. I also connect with a friend that I have not seen in a while or do something with our family. I also read, but no fiction. Praise music on Pandora on my phone is something I love while I walk, run, or ride my bike.

It was on one of those Sundays, walking and listening to praise music that I felt the Lord was calling me to write this book. If I had not been intentional in my pursuit of a sabbath, I would not have heard that call, because I would have been listening to a fictional book. Listening to fictional books is not a bad thing, I just find that for me, I need to do without it for a day and use that time to be open to the promptings of the Holy Spirit.

Searching for ways to rest in the Lord, remains a struggle for me. That is probably why this is the shortest chapter in this book. I obviously do not have many answers. I am truly a work without much progress in this area. If you, like me, struggle with this, I hope something in this chapter has been helpful for you. Perhaps, the best advice of all comes straight from Jesus, "Come to me all of you who are tired from carrying heavy loads, and I will give you rest. Take my yoke and put it on you and learn from me because I am gentle and humble in spirit; and you will find rest."[105]

---

[105] *TEV*, Matthew 11; 28, 29

Seek His Presence

"You will seek me and find me when you seek me with all your heart."[106]
-Jeremiah

This quote above made over 2500 years ago by the prophet Jeremiah lays the responsibility of seeking God clearly on us. The verb "seek" is an active verb. God has promised always to be with us. Jesus says, "And surely I am with you always, to the very end of the age." [107]

God is omnipresent. He is always near to everything. We can trust in that promise, but we are told in many different places in the Bible to seek the Lord. So, what does that mean?

In an article in Desiring God, John Piper says, "Both the Old and New Testaments say it is a setting of the mind and heart on God. It is the conscious fixing or focusing of our mind's attention and our heart's affection on God."[108]

He wants us to be actively involved in seeking his presence. He is available to all, but we must take the initiative in developing a relationship. God desires us to search for him.

---

[106] *NIV*, Jeremiah 29:13
[107] *NIV*, Matthew. 28:20b
[108] https://www.desiringgod.org/articles/what-does-it-mean-to-seek-the-lord

What does focus on God involve? There are so many distractions in our lives, focusing on anything is a challenge. For me, it must be my first thought of the day as I wake up. I am a morning person, and I am more alert when I first wake up. For those who are not morning people, pick a time that works for you and schedule your time with the Lord as an appointment.

The hour of the day is unimportant, but consistency is. I have my Bible app all set up on my phone, so I do not have to search for what I want to read. Then I have my *Daily Guideposts* close at hand. I like to read both devotional and then actual Bible verses.

If time is rushed, the Bible app will read the plan that you have selected to you. Because this book is about what I wish I could always do, I must admit, that I do not always make this appointment with the Lord, but it is something at which I attempt to be consistent. I certainly know that when I do read or listen, everything goes much more smoothly.

There is no right or wrong way to seek the Lord. We were all created with unique personalities, learning styles and gifts. For many years, I tried to fit myself into a mold of seeking God that was not a good fit for me. All it did was frustrate me, and I felt like I could never develop a relationship with the Lord.

In His book called, *Sacred Pathways,*[109] Gary Thomas talks about nine ways that one can connect with the Lord.

They are below:

Sacred Pathways

Naturalist	find God in nature
Ascetic	is drawn to a disciplined life
Traditionalist	loves historical liturgies
Activist	comes alive spiritually with a great cause
Caregiver	meets God in serving
Sensate	senses God through five senses
Enthusiast	loves to grow through people
Contemplative	is drawn to solidarity reflection and prayer
Intellectual	loves God by learning

[109] Thomas, Gary, *Sacred Pathways: Nine Ways to Connect with God,* Grand Rapids, Zondervan, 2020

When I read these, it was very freeing. I realized that I am an intellectual in the way that I connect with the Lord. The term frightened me because I do not think of myself as an intellectual. However, I do love to read and learn about God. I am happiest when I am preparing a lesson or even doing the research to write this book. It was also clear what pathways are not for me. I love people, so enthusiast would also fit, as would naturalist but none of the others work very well for me. The important thing is to find your pathway and develop a plan on how you will seek the Lord.

John Maxwell tells us that to have an intimate relationship with the Lord, there are three foundations we must understand, 1) Intimacy with God is not automatic, a result of right choices, 2) Intimacy with God begins with our own submission, humility, and brokenness, and 3) We naturally oppose God and must make our move toward him.[110]

God is always there for us, but we choose the depth of our relationship. As you know from the story of my conversion, I left the Lord for several years. He was always there waiting patiently for me to return, but I had to choose to return to him. I had to submit and release my control to him (Something I have done many times more.) It is so easy to focus on our accomplishments and not acknowledge from whence they have come.

---

[110] Maxell, John, *One Hour with God, Weekly Plan for Spiritual Growth,* "Intimacy with God," Atlanta, Injoy, 1994.

Denying the Lord is simple and extremely easy. It requires no work on your part. However, it is ever so challenging to show your faith by your actions. Just accept now that despite your good intentions, you will fail.

Jesus tells us, "But seek his kingdom first and his righteousness and all these things will be given to you as well."[111] So, to what do the words "these things" in the above quote refer? We look back at the previous verses in Chapter Six in this book and see that Jesus is telling us not to worry about anything.

Our heavenly father knows what we need and will provide it. Jesus further says, "Therefore, do not worry, for tomorrow will worry about itself. Each day has enough troubles of its own."[112] That says to me that when we focus on the Lord, everything that we worry about passes. When we are seeking his kingdom, everything else falls away.

Worry is like a rocking chair. It keeps moving as long as you pump it but does not get you anywhere. Worry robs you of your peace and can cause major health issues. Most things about which we worry, we have no effect on changing.

We need to get out of our rocking chair and start moving. All worry does is hamper our forward motion. Sometimes, that inertia just stops us from ever getting moving. If worry is something that plagues you, really read the Bible.

---

111 *NIV,* Matthew 6:33
112 *Ibid,* Matthew 6:34

Read how God has been in the rescuing mode for thousands of years. And know that he can rescue you, too. This does not mean we should try to push everything off on God. I have known people who would wait forever and not get anything done. One of my favorite expressions is," not even God can steer a parked car."

To be steered, the car must be in motion or at least out of park. Have you ever known someone who uses waiting on the Lord as an excuse? God wants us to seek him and try to discern his will for us. However, God is also willing to let us take the wheel. He will let us drive until we ask for help. When we know we need help, we need to humble ourselves and ask for his help.

Seeking God should be as urgent as looking for a lost valuable possession. I wear a beautiful diamond ring with two stones. I inherited the larger one from my aunt. For years, I did not know what to do with it. I already had an engagement ring with a beautiful but smaller diamond.

For our twenty-fifth wedding anniversary, my husband and I had a setting designed so that I could wear both diamonds. Both diamonds were in a six-prong tiffany setting. It was a beautiful ring. At that time, I operated a swim school in Southern California.

On a particular day, I was leading the early morning Bible study we called, The Early Word. (More about that in the chapter on Study) I got up early to make the coffee, sat down to say a quick prayer and noticed my ring while my hands were folded in my lap. Staring at me was a large empty gap surrounded by six prongs. I cannot begin to tell you how ugly it looked to me.

At first, I was most dismayed to put it mildly. I asked for prayer to find the diamond. After the group left, my husband and I tore the bed apart. We searched the house high and low but to no avail. I decided that it was just a thing and I had to give it up.

Besides, it was a busy day and I had to give a speech that night at the University of Southern California. That did not stop me from ruminating about it all day and going through all my previous day's steps. Rather than getting directions on how to drive to USC, I just started driving thinking I already knew how to get there. Well, I did not.

Driving and being preoccupied with thoughts about where my diamond could be. suddenly I realized, I was going out of my way. Instead of going the more direct route, I found myself driving by the YWCA where I had taught swim classes the night before. I was still ahead of schedule and decided to stop in and see if I had lost the stone in the locker room.

I stopped by the pool to ask the teacher if she had seen it. To talk to her, I looked down at the pool. Wow! There it was brightly shining up at me about an inch from the drain. I had a vision of that time long ago when I sat by the sea and saw the glimmering rising sun making the water sparkle like many diamonds. I just really wanted one back. The teacher dove under and retrieved it for me. It was a miracle to still be there. The pool was small and shallow, and anyone could have kicked it unintentionally into the drain.

To put it mildly, I was ecstatic. This is all to illustrate trust in the Lord and seek with all your heart. I prayed to find that lost gem, but I also went into action. I thought about nothing else but where that diamond could be. Then I accepted the situation and let the Lord lead me. Just think about what could happen if I would always seek the Lord with that kind of focus?

Serve

"No one should seek their own good, but the good of others."
-Apostle Paul[113]

Many times, when we think of service, we think of someone exceptionally well known for their service to others, a person like Mother Theresa. As we all know, she was a woman who dedicated her life to serving others. Rather thinking of a well-known international person like Mother Theresa, we might think of an individual in our local community who is well known for their service.

We might also think of a church member who stands out as a person of service. Thinking of all these great super stars of service, we tend to become intimidated. We begin to wonder how we could ever be able to serve such as these.

First, let us get a clear picture of what it means to serve. An article from South Bay Church[114], talks about a study by the Pew Research Center [115] that found that "roughly two-thirds of highly religious adults (65%) say they have donated money, time or goods to help the poor in the past week, compared with only 41% who are less religious."

---

[113] NIV, I Corinthians 10:24

[114] https://www.southbaychurchli.org/life-purpose-hope-blog/why-we-serve
[115] https://www.pewforum.org/2016/04/12/religion-in-everyday-life/

South Bay church came up with four reasons why we should serve.

1. We serve because Jesus served.
2. We are all given gifts to use.
3. We are parts of the whole.
4. We serve to bring glory to God.

Thank you to South Bay Church. Here is my take on their four reasons.

First - We serve because Jesus served – The greatest servant of all was Jesus. There are examples throughout the New Testament of him serving, feeding large groups, visiting, and healing the sick, forgiving sin, restoring sight to the blind, teaching the gospel, bringing the dead back to life, giving hope to the hopeless and most importantly giving his life for us. There, again, we cannot begin to compare, but we can draw from some specific instructions on how to serve in Matthew 25. Rather than try to pull out a verse, I think it is important to quote the whole section.

[34] "Then the King will say to those on his right, 'Come, you who are blessed by my Father; take your inheritance, the kingdom prepared for you since the creation of the world. [35] For I was hungry, and you gave me something to eat, I was thirsty, and you gave me something to drink, I was a stranger and you invited me in, [36] I needed clothes and you clothed me, I was sick and you looked after me, I was in prison and you came to visit me. [37] "Then the righteous will answer him, 'Lord, when did we see you hungry and feed you, or thirsty and give you something to drink? [38] When did we see you a stranger and invite you in, or needing clothes and clothe you? [39] When did we see you sick or in prison and go to visit you? [40] "The King will reply, 'Truly I tell you, whatever you did for one of the least of these brothers and sisters of mine, you did for me.'[116]

Jesus was clear that all his followers must serve. It is in the story of the last supper shared in the Gospel of John. Jesus wraps a towel around his waist and begins to wash the feet of his disciples. Since all wore sandals and traveled over dusty roads, feet got very dirty and this was an especially gross task, usually undertaken by a servant. After washing his disciples' feet, Jesus said, "I have given you an example to follow. Do as I have done to you."[117] There can be no doubt that Jesus was a servant.

---

[116] *NIV,* Matthew 25: 35 -40
[117] *NLT,* John 13: 14 - 15

Second - We are all given gifts to use - As indicated previously, we are all unique individuals created by God for his purpose. As such we have each been given our own gifts. Sources differ on the number of gifts given to us by the Lord. There are at least eight passages in the Bible listing one or more of the spiritual gifts.

Since there are so many differences of opinion, I am going to go with what my church teaches in the Spiritual Gifts class I took there. There are twenty-three spiritual gifts.[118]

An internet search will help you identify all of the gifts and these gifts are discussed further in the chapter in this book entitled, Set the Example. Spiritual gifts may or may not remain consistent throughout your life. Over the years, some of mine have changed. The last time I took an assessment my top three were: leadership, evangelism, and hospitality.

Evangelism did not even appear in my list the first time I took the assessment over twenty years ago. Serving and using our gifts will look like something different for each of us. The most important thing is to use our gifts.

Sometimes using our gifts is a just matter of what we can do at the time. Carol Knapp tells a story in *Guideposts* about walking daily and meeting up with a man and his dog, Little Missy.[119] They met many times and exchanged greetings.

---

[118] Grove Community Church, Spiritual Gifts, Riverside, CA, attn. Joe Hobbs
[119] Knapp, Carol, *Daily Guideposts 2021,* "January 8, 2021", Danbury CT,

One day the man was not there, and Carol found out he was sick. Shortly after, he was confined to a bed. Carol decided she would walk the dog daily. She saw a need and filled it. This was not an earth-shaking service, but one that was desperately needed.

Third - We are parts of the whole – none of us operates in a vacuum. Just as we are each given gifts, those gifts are part of a larger whole. This was explained by Paul in his letter to the Romans, "For just as each of us has one body with many members, and these members do not all have the same function, so in Christ we, though many, form one body, and each member belongs to all the others."[120] Here Paul uses the concept of the human body to teach how we should live and work together. No part of the body is more important than any other. Carrying that over to serving, no service is more important than any other. Going back to the previous dog walking example, Carol. walking the dog was just as important as the physician who treated the sick man. All were needed for his well-being. What is important is to do what you see as a need. You may be the only one to recognize that need.

Guideposts, 2021, p. 9
[120] *NIV,* Romans 12:4-5.

Fourth - We serve to bring glory to God – when we serve as we have been gifted, we bring glory to God. In the book of First Peter, it says, "Each of you should use whatever gift you have received to serve others, as faithful stewards of God's grace in its various forms.... so that in all things God may be praised through Jesus Christ."[121] Bringing glory to God should be what life is all about. How can you up your game in serving your spouse, family, friends, neighbors, coworkers, people with urgent needs? Spend some time praying and asking the Lord to show you where to join Him in serving others for their good and for his glory. When you feel that quiet nudge in your spirit that tells you to call a friend, volunteer for something, send a card or whatever, that is from the Lord. Just do it.

---

[121] *NIV*, 1 Peter 4:11 – 12

Set the Example

"Whatever you do or say, do it as a representative of the Lord Jesus."

-Paul, the Apostle[122]

Several years ago, I read an article about the late Billy Graham, arguably one of the greatest evangelists ever. Once when he was asked, "are you a Christian?" Billy Graham responded with, "I try to be." That gave me a lot of hope because there are days that I feel I need to try much harder than others. I got a great Mother's Day card from my daughter, extolling what she thought were my virtues. In her adjectives, she listed Godly and then added in parenthesis, most of the time. I loved it because it just shows that I am still a work in progress.

"Preach the Gospel at all times. When necessary, use words," is often attributed to St. Francis of Assisi. Whether he said this or not, I love the picture it paints in my mind. The point is that I could be the only Christian that some people will ever see. Therefore, I often ask myself these important questions; how am I living my life, am I living it to the glory of God, am I living as a representative of the Lord Jesus? I also ask myself, will people be drawn to the Lord because of my lifestyle?

---

[122] Colossians 3:17

In my opinion, that is an impossible standard for me. That is why God sacrificed his only son to save me from my wrongdoings. I understand that I must strive to do my best, even though I will never be perfect. I must not compare myself to others, but rather strive to be more like God.

One morning, when I was up early sitting outside, there was a bunch of what looked like ordinary blackbirds roosting in the trees. As the day was breaking, I was overcome by the beauty of the various tunes of those simple birds. They all looked the same from a distance, but each of them was singing a slightly different tune. It occurred to me that we humans are just like those birds.

All of us have a different song to sing, a song that has been given to us by our creator. Only you can sing that song, and no one else can do it as well as you. My notes have changed over the years as I have grown in my faith and God willing, they will continue to change as I grow and change. I imagine that your song is yet to be sung.

We humans have been given gifts by our creator to use to build up the family of God. It is according to God's grace that we have been given these gifts. We had nothing to do with what these gifts are. In a letter to the Romans, we are instructed by Paul to not think more highly of ourselves because we have these gifts, but rather to be modest in our thinking and judge ourselves according to the amount of faith that God has given us.[123] All of our gifts are important to God's community of faith, and we must each perform according to gifts we have been given. As we present our bodies to God as a living sacrifice, we are to be a blessing to others using those gifts with which we have been blessed.

All humans have gifts not so much for our sake, but for the sake of others. A gift is not a gift unless it is given to someone else. We are like the apple tree which produces fruit, not for its own consumption but for the consumption of others. The Lord has given you gifts so that you can bless others by ministering to them. The life of discipleship comes not in isolation, but in the process of ministering to others. So, what are these gifts, how do we get them, and how do we use them?

[123] *NIV,* Romans 12:3

Paul lists 7 gifts in Romans 12, which are: prophesying, serving, teaching, encouraging, contributing to other's needs (sharing) leadership, and showing mercy. Throughout the New Testament there are a total of 23 specific gifts and then others that can be deduced. If you do not know what yours are, you can take a spiritual gifts test or take a class. Try Googling it and see how many websites there are. A great reference is listed here in the footnotes.[124] There is also another way. What makes you feel good to do for the body of Christ (or for an individual person)? Well, that is probably your spiritual gift.

Our spiritual gifts may or may not be our talents. For example, a person who is a teacher by profession may have the spiritual gift of hospitality and not the spiritual gift of teaching. If you have the gift of teaching, you have it so others can be taught spiritual truths. If you have the gift of mercy, you have it because there are so many who are afflicted, but you may or may not be in the nursing profession. If you have the gift of prophesying, it is because someone needs to hear the truth. If you have the gift of encouraging, it is because so many are in need of a word of hope. What have you been given that you can use for the body of Christ?

---

[124] https://spiritualgiftstest.com/spiritual-gifts/

Let's go back to the quote that begins this chapter. "Whatever you do or say, do it as a representative of the Lord Jesus. "How am I using the gifts given to me? Do I continually use the gifts with which I have been blessed to be a role model for others? Am I representing the Lord Jesus in all that I do? Most times, my answer would be like Billy Graham's. My answer would be, "I try, but I don't always make it."

Study

"Faith is not an achievement; it is a gift. It comes through the hearing and study of the word."

-Martin Luther

In a book called *Friendish*,[125] author, Kelly Needham, talks about the three ways that God has given us to draw near to him: reading our Bible, praying, and being a part of a local church. I have covered praying and being a part of a local church previously.

Why is it so important to study God's Word to draw near to him? The first step in getting to know someone is to gather information about that person. On that day when I gave up my control and surrendered to Christ, not only was I filled with great joy, but also with an insatiable desire to learn more. To that point, I had never engaged in serious Bible study. My pastor, Bill Johnson, suggested that the best way to learn was to teach a Bible Study.

At that time, my schedule was incredibly jammed. I had to be creative and enlisted a few fellow church members to join me for what we eventually called, The Early Word, beginning at 6 AM on Wednesdays. Since I was so new to Bible Study, much less leading it, I readily accepted Bill's suggestion that I begin with the book of Isaiah.

---

[125] Needham, Kelly, Friendish, Nelson Books, Nashville, TN, 2019

I had no idea that it was one of the tougher books to study. Thanks, a lot, Bill. I also did not know at that time that two of my spiritual gifts are leadership and teaching. Had I known that I could have relaxed and let God take the wheel a bit more. Being so new, I did have to rely on the Lord for help in teaching and digging into Isaiah.

Armed with a new study Bible, a study guide, a leaders' guide, and a commentary, I began what would be a lifelong journey of learning. Why lifelong? There are so many truths to apply, and those truths are applicable at different times in your life. So many times, I have read a passage familiar to me and found something I had not noticed before. Study is not just some intellectual game played by a few, but it is transformational in our lives. We are either growing or dying. There is no standing still.

The apostle Paul said, "Do not conform to the pattern of this world but be transformed by the renewing of your mind. Then you will be able to test and approve what God's will is – his good and perfect will."[126] How do I learn the will of God in my life? I learn by reading and studying his Word. I love that word, "transformed." How wonderful to think that by reading and applying his Word, I can transform to be a little more of what he has intended for me.

---

[126] Ibid, p. 2481

The aim of study for a Christian is to seek a deeper transformation of our hearts and lives. Christian study has two parts. The first is being informed of the truth through information, interpreting and evaluating. The second is being formed in the truth through the regular application, reflection, and growing in love for the subject being studied. We study Christ so that we can be conformed to Christ.

Study is a spiritual discipline. It's the discipline of continual discovery and the exercise of faith seeking understanding. Through study, our patterns of thinking and living change and expand to accommodate greater truth, the mind, and the way of Christ. Through study, we exchange destructive habits for new, life-giving, ways of thinking, and living.

If it is a spiritual discipline, how do we acquire it? We need to have a plan in place. If there is no plan, every excuse will get in the way. For me, it must be done in the morning. I am a morning person, so I do not get as distracted. Also, it is easier for my mind to focus. The important thing is to just begin. Enlist a spouse or friend to do it with you and then be accountable for doing it. There are many daily devotional books that have a verse and then a devotion that goes with that verse. I have been an avid reader of *Daily Guideposts* produced through Guideposts for many years. That devotion comes in both print and an online version.

What then should we study? The choices are limitless. Study may be done by the study of a book of the Bible or through topical study. As previously mentioned in the chapter on accountability, the Bible App is great to have on your phone. You can read or listen to various translations depending on your learning style. You can pick the study, and it gives you the reading or readings each day. It is easy to track your progress.

A great overview of the books of the Bible can be found online through *The Bible Project.com.*[127] The *Bible Project* is a free site and can be found on *YouTube*. A definition of what the *Bible Project* is comes from their website, "Bible is one unified story that leads to Jesus, but we don't always treat it that way. At Bible Project, we make animated videos that explore the books and themes of the Bible." Another website, *Bible Gateway.com*[128] is a tremendous resource. The *Bible Gateway,* too, has many translations available and it can also be in audio form. These are just a few of the thousands of resources available today for Bible study. With so many ways to study, why is it so hard to do? These are the excuses that I have heard and used myself. Hopefully, this gives you ideas on how you can begin Bible study and some of the things that may have been holding you back.

[127] https://bibleproject.com/
[128] https://www.biblegateway.com/

The main thing is to start. Grab a friend or talk to someone at your church. We must be intentional if we are to grow in grace in the image of God and the mind of Christ.

Excuses	Solutions
"I don't have time."	Get real. No one has time today. Each day comes with 1440 minutes. Would it be fair to give God ten of those?
"I don't know what to study."	Ask for help. Join a Bible study. Find out what your pastor will be preaching about and study that.
"I don't like to read."	Try other ways (Internet, audio and video recordings and films, webcasts, join a discussion group).
"I don't understand parts of the Bible."	Welcome to the club, or I could say, "Duh! That is why we study." The most important part is just to begin. As you study more, some passages become clearer.

Tell Others

"Every testimony is valid because there is someone out there a lot like you."
-Greg Laurie[129]

Several years ago, I was searching for material for a Bible study I was leading. I took a book off the shelf to check it out. I was not interested in that book, but as I started to put it back, a book nearby caught my attention. It was by one of my favorite authors, Bill Hybels. I was about two weeks away from giving a workshop on evangelism. The book, *A Walk Across the Room,*[130] has become one of my favorites, and it seemed like the book was put right in front of me when I most needed it. Hybels says, "Life's greatest moments evolve from simple acts of cooperating with God's mysterious promptings." [131] The book really impacted me because it talked about the simple things that we can do. The most important thing is just being open to those quiet promptings that come from God that say we need to talk about him to others.

---

[129] Laurie, Greg, *Tell Someone: You Can share the Good News*, Nashville: B & H Publishers, A Division of Lifeway
[130] Hybels, Bill, *A Walk Across the Room,* Grand Rapids Michigan: Zondervan, 2006
[131] Ibid, p. 16

The title of the book comes from an experience that Hybels had with a former Muslim who had been at a luncheon with Hybels. As a pastor of a mega church, Hybels assumed he would not have much in common with the man who appeared to be Muslim. From across the room, the man mouthed to Hybels, "I love your books." After lunch, Hybels walked over, and the man told him his story. The man had become accustomed to being ostracized at many events due to his beliefs. He was at an event, attending as a man who was obviously of the Muslim faith. A stranger walked up to him and just started a conversation.

That initial conversation led to a friendship which later led to the Muslim giving his life to Christ. The stranger had to walk across a room, start a conversation, and see where it went. Maybe you are reading this book, because someone took a chance and started a conversation with you about the Lord. For me, this would not be due to just one conversation but many conversations by many people. Each one got me just a little closer to establishing my own relationship with Jesus. In his book, *Evangelism without Additives*,[132] Jim Henderson states that it takes about two years for people to move from seeker to finder and from being missed to seeking the missed. It is a gradual process, not an isolated event.

---

[132] Henderson, Jim, *Evangelism without Additives*, New York: Waterbook, a Division of Penguin Random House, 2007

I remember vividly the first time someone asked me about my beliefs. I was totally unprepared. A few years after I finally committed my life to Christ, I was standing at a table full of food happily munching on something. A business associate who was also becoming a good friend asked me out of the blue, "So why do you and Dick go to church?" There it was…the scariest question on the planet. I said a quick prayer. I cannot even remember how I answered her, but I did have the presence of mind to ask her and her family to join us in attending our church. They did and they kept coming.

I wish I could say that I was instrumental in her finally committing her life to Christ, but I passed it off to our pastor and encouraged her to take a class called "Disciple." We also sponsored her and her husband on a spiritual retreat called, *The Walk to Emmaus.* She finally did make the commitment, but not due to any great efforts on my part. Yes, I did get her pointed in the right direction and I prayed for her. However, what she really wanted to know was what kind of an impact having Christ as my savior had in my life. I just did not get that. I thought if I pointed her in the right direction, she would get it for herself. I tell you this story, because I think many of us are just plain fearful when it comes to sharing Jesus with others. We are scared that we will mess it up. We do not know what to say, or we hope someone else will do it for us.

The key to knowing what to say is preparation. New followers of Christ are so excited about what has just happened to them, they just blurt it out and they are highly effective at telling their story. Then a strange phenomenon happens. Hybels states, "The longer a person attends church, the fewer evangelistic discussions they engage in with family members and friends."[133]

I think this is just because this is not foremost on their mind and because they are unprepared. It is also because they start hanging around with people who believe as they do. The apostle, Peter, gives us truly clear instructions on being prepared. He says, "But have reverence for Christ in your hearts, and honor him as Lord. Be ready at all times to answer anyone who asks you to explain the hope that you have in you but do it with great gentleness and respect."[134]

---

[133] Hybels, Bill, *A Walk Across the Room,* Grand Rapids Michigan: Zondervan, 2006, p 61
[134] TEV, 1 Peter 3:15-16

Notice it says, be ready to share with anyone who asks. That does not mean to go out and cram it down someone. That is what gives sharing the Gospel a bad name. When someone starts asking you questions of a spiritual nature, that is when they are ready. Then you need to be ready. It is this "be ready" part on which I would like to focus on for the remainder of this chapter. Here is the best part. You do not have to be good. It is your story, and you can tell it however is best for you.

You heard my story in the chapter on Grace in this book. I have told it many times, so that is the practice part. Write it down and then get familiar with it. If you are part of a small group or Bible study, ask if you might practice by sharing it with them.

You will want to tell your story in a way that is appealing to people and not turn them off. Bill Hybels says that you should be able to tell it in 45 seconds or less. Others say two to three minutes is fine. People tend to shut down if you get long winded. In addition to being short, it should also be clear, avoid religious words or freaky things, and be full of humility.

Your story is not to pass judgement on anyone else, but simply to share what you have found. You need to tell people where you were before you came to Christ and how you changed afterwards. Some stories will have a dramatic conversion. For many others, it has simply been a matter of following Christ all their lives and how that has been for them. Whatever is your story, it is yours and you are the only one who can tell that story. Someone needs to hear it from you. You just need to make it known.

My church did a whole year with the theme of "Make It Known." The objective was to equip every church member with the ability to be able to share their story. Two of the staff members wrote a wonderful song to celebrate this theme. I am grateful that they have given me permission to use their lyrics.

The song can be found on Amazon.[135]

Make It Known –

featuring Jenni Price & Brandon Stoppe, Grove Community Church

Verse 1

"Wonderful things You have done
Wonderful things you will do
Father we gather as one
Waiting to hear from you.

Pre-Chorus

Spirit unite our lives
Fix our lives
Show us the weight of Your grace
As we seek your ways

---

[135] https://www.amazon.com/s?k=Make+It+known+by+Stoppe+and+Price&ref=nb_sb_noss

Chorus
Make it known
In the depths of our hearts
Make it known
Shine Your light in the dark
Make it known
Who You are
Make it known
To the ends of the earth
Make it known
Till the nations have heard
Make it known
Make it known
Make it known

Verse 2
Wonderful things You have done
Wonderful things You will do
Sending your only son
Jesus the way and the truth
Bridge
Spend us for your glory
All we offer you
Every breath for you
Jesus You are worthy
You have made it known
Spend us for your glory
All we offer you

This song says it so clearly. If you are a Christian, you have a responsibility to "Make it known." There are many fabulous books written to help you go further to share the gospel with others. Many are in the footnotes listed as you read through this chapter. Others follow here. In addition, there are many great websites which you can just Google. The main purpose of this chapter is just to encourage you to know your story and be ready to "make it known."

Great references for Telling Others

Barnes, Mike, *Which Way is the Ocean?* Riverside, CA: Grove
   Community Church, 2010.

Feldmeir, Mark, *You Need to Get Out More*, 2012, Available on
   Amazon.

Gilbert, Greg, *What Is the Gospel?* Wheaton, IL: Crossway,
   2010.

Hybels, Bill and Mittleberg, Mark, *Becoming a Contagious
   Christian,* Grand Rapids, MI, 1994.

Ingram, Chip, *Share the Love: How to Talk to Anyone about
   God,* Living on the Edge with Chip Ingram, Inc., 2019.

Treat Your Body as a Temple

"Do you not know that your bodies are temples of the Holy Spirit, who is in you, whom you have received from God? You are not your own; you were bought at a price. Therefore, honor God with your bodies."[136]

–Apostle Paul

First, what does it mean to think of your body as a temple of the Holy Spirit? Let us go back to the time when this was written. Commentators believe that the letter to the Corinthians was written in approximately 55 AD. As Paul was writing, I can imagine that he was thinking of the splendor and grandeur of Herod's temple in Jerusalem which was still standing.

Having seen a scaled down version of the temple when I visited Jerusalem, I can only wonder at what a spectacle it must have been. It was there that the Hebrews went to worship God. This picture gives an inkling of the magnificence of that edifice.

---

[136]The Holy Bible, 1 Corinthians 6:19-20

When Jesus died, was resurrected, and finally ascended to heaven, he left his Holy Spirit indwelling in us. This is detailed in the book of Acts. In it, Peter said, "Repent and be baptized, every one of you, in the name of Jesus Christ for the forgiveness of your sins. And you will receive the gift of the Holy Spirit." [137]

To have that spirit of God within us means that it is in our bodies (temples) in which God resides. If we really took that to heart, would we do a better job of caring for our bodies?

Let's imagine for a moment that a friend has given you the care of a thoroughbred racehorse worth millions. Would you keep that horse up late with caffeine, feed it junk food, and never exercise it? Of course, you would not. You would care for it better than yourself. Why is it then that we have so much trouble caring for ourselves?

The CDC states that 90% of the nation's $3.5 trillion in annual health care expenditures are for people with chronic and mental health conditions.

Those chronic conditions are listed as heart disease and stroke, cancer, diabetes, obesity, arthritis, Alzheimer's, and even tooth decay.[138] Although heredity plays a factor, some of these are lifestyle choices and therefore preventable.

---

[137] *Ibid*, Acts 2:38
[138] https://www.cdc.gov/chronicdisease/about/costs/index.htm

Using the word TEMPLE as an acronym, let us consider how we might be able to use our bodies as a temple.

T   **Take supplements**

E   **Eat right**

M   **Maintain a healthy weight**

P   **Prepare your mind**

L   **Leave time for rest**

E   **Exercise**

Take Supplements – Reversing its previous position against vitamins in 2002, the Journal of American Medicine said that all Americans should take a multivitamin/ multimineral.[139] Why is this?

Most people do not consume an optimal amount of all vitamins by diet alone. In a Phytonutrient Report commissioned by the Nutrilite Health Institute, it states that "A majority of adults worldwide fail to consume the minimum quantity of fruits and vegetables recommended by the World Health Organization.

---

[139] https://jamanetwork.com/journals/jama/fullarticle/195039

Most would have to at least double their current consumption to meet the minimum global recommendation."[140] Obstacles to eating fruits and vegetables may include busy lives, cost, and seasonal and geographic availability." [141] As a society, we are enamored with fast food and doing everything on the go.

In addition, even the healthy food that we eat is not as nutrient rich as it was even fifty years ago. Farming practices are not what they were, and there has been a gradual loss of topsoil. When I was growing up in the late fifties and early sixties, the topsoil was about 21 inches.

Today that topsoil is only 7 inches. This is greatly reducing the amount of nutrients in the soil. We are also getting produce from all over the world. That product is picked ahead of optimal nutrient time and preserved. When it finally reaches our kitchens, some of the nutrition is gone.

All this is to say that you should take a multivitamin. There are so many, how do you choose? Vitamins are not regulated by the FDA, so choose one from a reputable manufacturer who has secured independent testing.

[140] https://www.amwayglobal.com/wp-content/uploads/2017/09/global_phytonutrient_report_commissioned_by_the_nutrilite_health_institute.pdf
[141] https://files.marcomcentral.app.pti.com/amway/Nutrilite%20Keep/nutr-nut-fact-v-en--GlobalPhytonutrientReportFAQ.pdf

Since you are trying to supplement what you do not eat, the most important thing to consider is that it be plant based and come from a wide variety of plants. The manufacturer should also give you a money back guarantee.

For more information, there is an excellent book called, *The Secrets of Supplements* [142].

Eat Right – We hear this all the time, but what does it really mean? Most of us know what healthy food is. We just struggle with choosing healthy food. Why is that? To me, the simplest explanation is convenience. When we are hungry, we don't always make the best choices. Whatever you can find fast to stuff in your mouth is what usually happens. That means we need to food-prep healthy foods so that when we are hungry, we reach for those.

The Harvard School of Medicine has a great chart of a plate.[143] The plate is divided into 4 segments with whole grains being 25%, lean protein 25%, vegetables 35%, and fruits 15%. I love it, because it is very visual. Outside the plate are suggestions on drinking water and healthy oils. Dairy is limited to 1 – 2 servings per day. It is a great guide to healthy eating. You can also find great information on healthy eating and recipes on their website.

---

[142] Askew, Gloria and Paquette, Jerre, *The Secrets of Supplements,* Phyte Media, 2008
[143] https://www.health.harvard.edu/staying-healthy/healthy-eating-plate

A remarkably simple way to make certain that you are getting a wide variety of fruits and vegetables, is to eat by color. Try to eat two of every color each day; 2 reds, 2 purple/blues, 2 orange/yellows, 2 whites and 2 greens. That will give you a wide variety of phytonutrients. Phytonutrients are those nutrients which give the plant, fruit or vegetable it's color and nutrition. It just makes good sense to eat as wide a variety as possible to get the most diverse benefits. Keep a list of what you eat in a week and note the color (s) that you are not as good at eating. Those would be what you need to supplement.

Maintain a Healthy Weight – In 2016, CBS reported the following statistics from the Center for Disease Control, "the average weight of men in the United States rose from 181 pounds to 196 pounds between 1988-1994 and 2011-2014. Their average height remained the same at about 5 feet, 9 inches. The average woman, meanwhile, expanded from 152 pounds to 169 pounds while her height remained steady at just under 5 feet, 4 inches." [144] The article goes on to list what the causes might be and then concludes that we, as a nation, are consuming more calories than we burn. Maintaining a healthy weight is not rocket science. One has to eat less and move more.

---

[144] https://www.cbsnews.com/news/americans-weight-gain-since-1980s-startling/

Prepare Your Mind – As I am writing this, our country is seven months into a pandemic. Over 200,000 Americans have died. Our lives have changed drastically, and we have a very important election before us. Unrest is high, and our nation is very divided. If you focus on what the media is reporting, all the news is very bleak. It seems the networks are in a contest to see who can give the most depressing news. Who wants to be exposed to all the negativity that is reported? As you now know from a previous chapter, I watch neither the news nor network TV. This enables me to stay focused on the positive. I want to only put positivity in my mind and speak in a positive way about myself and others. Really studying God's Word is the best way to feed your mind.

This quote, which bears repeating, from the Apostle Paul remains a terrific way to prepare your mind to be a temple for the Lord. Quoting from his letter to the Philippians; "Finally my brothers and sisters, whatever is true, whatever is noble, whatever is right, whatever is pure, whatever is lovely, whatever is admirable, - if anything is excellent or praiseworthy – think about such things."[145] If this was what we truly focused on, our minds would be a temple for the Lord.

---

[145] NIV, Philippians 4:8

Leave time for Rest – In the story of creation in the book of Genesis, it tells us that the Lord of the universe completed his work and rested. If after creating the earth, God took time to rest, why is it that I struggle so with resting? As previously stated, this is really a tough one for me. I am a high energy person who is very restless. I would rather be doing than resting. I have struggled with resting for most of my life.

Even though I know I need it, I would just rather not do it. A few years ago, I had a big wakeup call when I fell asleep at the wheel and drove into a huge bush in my neighborhood. I had just turned a corner, so thank heavens I was going very slow. My 3-year-old grandson was asleep in the car seat in the back. I woke up surrounded by bush in the front window. Talk about a scare! No one was hurt, but that bush did $13,000 worth of damage to my car.

That called for a huge adjustment in my life. Now I am very careful about when I drive, and I try to get more rest and if needed give myself a power nap during the day. I had all sorts of tests to see if anything was wrong. Nothing was found. I go so hard all day long. I think my body so longs for rest, that when I sit, I just fall asleep. Friends tell stories of me sleeping through all sorts of things that I really did not want to miss. Now I try to take a bit of time just to rest.

Exercise - It does not matter what you do for exercise. Do something you like; find a way to measure it; and find someone with whom to do it. Over the years, I have had several running partners, and I still have two friends with whom I love to run. Training for my first marathon, I had a close friend who showed up on my doorstep every Monday, Wednesday, and Friday. She had to show up and I had to be ready. We depended on each other. We ran that first marathon together and then two more. It was our dream to cross the finish line at the original marathon in Athens, Greece, and we did that. Even though I mostly run solo these days, I still sign up for a race to keep me focused and always having the next goal.

Treat your body as a temple and remember this acronym, TEMPLE. We are all a work in progress and want to be progressing toward good health all the time. It is well to remember," Good health is not a destination, but a series of small steps taken over a period of time."[146]

---

[146] Phillips, Jackie, Taken from a Teaching Series for Foster Care Kinship Programs at Riverside Community College

Worship

"Most middle-class Americans tend to worship their work, work at their play, and play at their worship."[147]

-John Maxwell

What comes to your mind when I say the word worship? I fear this quote by John Maxwell may be truer than we wish to admit. How do we truly worship? When we think of worship, we often refer to a type of music. Sometime the words praise, and worship are used interchangeably, but nothing could be further from the truth. Praise stems from recognizing the good acts of God but worship comes from the core of who the worshipper is and what God means to them.

Wikipedia defines worship as "Worship is an act of religious devotion usually directed towards a deity. For many, worship is not about an emotion, it is more about a recognition of God. An act of worship may be performed individually, in an informal or formal group, or by a designated leader. Such acts may involve honoring."[148] I love what my friend Carlos Huayanca says on the worship page of his church website, "Worship is not about playing an instrument or singing, it's about praising and honoring God with our witness"[149]

---

[147] Maxwell, John, *One Hour with God, Weekly Plan for Spiritual Growth,* Injoy, Inc, 1994
[148] https://en.wikipedia.org/wiki/Worship
[149] Huayanca, Carlos, https://calvarychapelinland.org/worship-ministry/

How do we go about praising and honoring God with our witness? We see many examples of individual worship in the Bible. Luke tells of an unnamed woman who lived a sinful life. She entered a house where Jesus was eating a meal with some church leaders. In those days, people reclined when eating meals, so Jesus was in a reclining position. The woman approached his feet. Overcome by his holiness, she wept and wet his feet with her tears. She then anointed his feet with an expensive perfume. Jesus was then criticized by the church leaders, but he praised the woman for her act of true worship. She was a witness to his holiness.[150]

The story of another unnamed woman in the Bible is told in the book of Mark.[151] Jesus was sitting outside the temple with his disciples. They were watching people make donations to the temple. Donations were collected in a large metal tube which made a big clunk when coins were dropped in. Everyone could tell who was making the largest donation by the clunking in the tube. There were many large donations that day, but along came a widow who made an exceedingly small donation. It was so small that it barely made a sound. Jesus praised her for this act. Others had given out of their abundance, but she gave all she had. This was an act of sacrificial worship.

---

[150] TEV, Luke 7:36 - 50

[151] TEV, Mark 12: 41 - 44

Both of those women were exhibiting different forms of worship, but each of them pleased the Lord, in their own way. We are told in the book of Hebrews, "Let us be thankful, then, because we receive a kingdom that cannot be shaken. Let us be grateful and worship God in a way that will please him, with reverence and awe."[152] That is all well and good, but what does that look like practically?

Rick Warren [153]tells us that worship should 1) involve your spirit and 2) should be thoughtful. Involving your spirit is not just singing some great songs but rather engaging your heart. It is a matter of connecting your spirit to God's. That can be done in many ways. Some of the ways, which are all found in various passages in the Bible, Warren suggests, are confessing, singing, shouting, standing in honor, kneeling, dancing, making a joyful noise, testifying, playing a musical instrument, and raising hands. All are perfectly welcome as an act of worship. What you choose depends upon your style and as discussed previously upon your spiritual pathway. Just as we all have different ways of seeking the Lord, we all have different ways to worship. What works for me might not work for you.

---

[152] TEV, Hebrews 12:28, p. 1101
[153] Warren, Rick, *The Purpose Driven Life,* Grand Rapids, MI: Zondervan, 2002, Chapter 13

The main thing is that we are in fellowship with the Lord. When we experience real worship, hearts and lives are changed. It is about getting to know the God who created us and coming to know Jesus in a real and meaningful manner. It is about experiencing the presence of the Lord in every aspect of our life not just on a particular day or in a particular place.

Worship should also be thoughtful. We are told to love God with all our mind four times in the Bible in both the Old and the New Testaments. We do not need superficial religious rituals. All we need is to be ready for the gentle prompts of the Spirit advising us through the reading and study of God's word. That is the most amazing thing about reading scripture. What you get from it is always changing. One thing builds on what you have already learned and your life experiences. All of that is constantly evolving. When you read, read different translations. It is amazing how a different word or words will increase your understanding. Some Bibles provide a more literal translation and others use more modern words.

When you shop for a Bible, find a knowledgeable person to assist you. There are so many different Bibles from which to choose. I volunteer at the bookstore at my church. Even as volunteers, we have taken a class on how to help people buy a Bible based on their interests and needs. You can also use a commentary to further your understanding.

So where should we worship? Where does not really matter. Some prefer corporate worship; others prefer to worship privately. Some will love a beautiful building and others feel God's spirit in a warehouse or at the beach. Some will enjoy worship in their homes on the television.

Any way you worship is important as it creates a personal relationship between God and you. Corporate worship can also help to bring a community together. Some people feel that they gain a better understanding of Christianity through attending services.

The most important thing is to create a time and a place. Find yours. For me, I love going to my church where I can worship in community with others. When we were quarantined due to the COVID-19 virus, I really missed worshipping at my church.

Soon my church and many others put their service online. It filled in the hole, but just was not the same. I also love walking, running, or riding my bike and listening to and singing along with some great praise music.

In his letter to the Romans, the apostle Paul says, "So then, my friends, because of God's great mercy to us I appeal to you: Offer yourselves as a living sacrifice to God, dedicated to his service and pleasing to him."[154]

---

[154] T*EV*, Romans 12:1

What does a living sacrifice involve? It involves sacrifice. It could be your time, energy, or your money, but it will involve giving something up. That could even be our self-centeredness. When our focus is on God, it is off ourselves. When we are not thinking about ourselves, it is easier to give our hearts to God. One of my most favorite Psalms, Psalm 100, [155] tells us how to enter joyfully into God's presence. To really savor this psalm, read several versions of it. His faithfulness extends to our generation and beyond.

Sing to the Lord, all the world
Worship the Lord with joy;
Come before him with happy songs!
Acknowledge that the Lord is God
He made us, and we belong to him;
We are his people; we are his flock.
Enter the temple gates with thanksgiving;
Go into his courts with praise.
Give thanks to him and praise him.
The Lord is good;
His love is eternal.
And his faithfulness lasts forever.
Let us praise and honor God with our witness.

---

[155] *Ibid,* Psalm 100

Faith

"I have fought the good fight, I have finished the race, I have kept the faith."

-Timothy[156]

As we come to this last and, in my opinion, the most important chapter. My prayer is that you will see some hope in all my faith struggles, and you will find peace about your struggles. Do I consider myself to be unfaithful? No! Do I struggle with my faith? Absolutely! It is far from perfect. I do pray that through all these struggles, my faith will continue to be strengthened. At the end of my days on this earth, I want to be able to say, "I have fought the good fight, I have finished the race, and I have kept the faith." This does not imply that every day my faith has been as strong as the last day, but it does say I stayed in the fight.

For me, as a marathoner, it is an image of a race. Any race will do, but for me it is a marathon. In the chapter on encouragement, I talked about the hardest part of running a marathon is the training. In that training, there are lots of ups and downs. As you are training and then finally running the race, sometimes endorphins kick in and it feels amazing. Then you "hit the wall," and you feel terrible.

---

[156] NIV, 2 Timothy 4:7

That is when you wonder why you ever decided to do this at all. I remember calling my husband asking to be picked up at the 18-mile mark one day during training. I was totally wiped out.

Sometimes you have a breakthrough, or maybe you do not have one and you just keep slugging through. Sometimes you stumble; other times you fall flat on your face and get some road rash. Sometimes being out there running is blissful; other times it is just plain painful. Finally, you near the finish line. At first, it is just what appears to be a mirage in the distance. Your spirits are lifted, and you may even pick up your pace. Then finishing becomes more real as you get closer.

My faith walk has been much like that. I am still running the race, but I am getting closer to the finish line. Some days I am full of faith with nary a doubt, and other days, it is just not as easy. Developing my faith has been a continual process but with starts and stops. I started with the faith of a child, lost that faith for many years, and then have gradually built it back up. The most amazing thing is that God stuck with me. Even though I left him, the God of my childhood never abandoned me. As I said in the chapter on Grace, he not only stuck with me, but he pursued me.

I have times when I feel really close to the Lord. Those I would call my faith highs or my mountain top experiences. Then there are times when I wonder if he is even listening. Humans are designed to go, share, and tell. To relate to others, we must experience both the highs and the lows.

There are all sorts of stumbling blocks to our faith. To get a broader perspective on those, I asked the members of the Facebook group for this book what were some of the stumbling blocks in their faith. Their answers were varied, but I am certain you will resonate with some of them. In no particular order, they are worry, knowing and clarifying God's plan, death and sickness in young people, trusting, letting go and letting God, discouragement, staying focused on God, listening to God, Christians judging, and Christians not being role models for their faith.

These are some of the things with which we struggle in our faith. So just what then is faith? There are lots of definitions, but I think the best comes from the book of Hebrews, Chapter 11. This is a whole chapter on faith and also gives a clear definition of faith. I really like the one from Today's English Version, "To have faith is to be sure of the things we hope for, to be certain of the things we cannot see." [157]

---

[157] Ibid, Hebrews 11:1

In that chapter, it extols the many saints who have shown great faith throughout the years. That is all well and good, but sometimes we need a modern person or persons of great faith.

I would love to share with you a story in modern times. The story is about Brother Yun and his wife, Deling. Yun was born in 1958 to a poor family in China. At the age of 16, he became a believer in Christ after a miracle healing of his father from cancer. Deling, also from an extremely poor family, became a follower of Christ at 18 after being healed of hemophilia. Yun was instrumental leading the house church movement in China and Deling was right by his side but not always physically.

Married only a short time, Yun became a fugitive because of his preaching the Gospel. He was imprisoned many times under wretched conditions, beaten, tortured, crippled, and healed. He even endured a 74 day fast while in prison.

Through his many trials and all these numerous imprisonments, he never wavered in his attempts to bring the Good News to everyone with whom he came in contact. Since Yun was in prison a lot, Deling was left as a single parent for much of their children's growing years. At one point, when they were both imprisoned at the same time, and their two children had to be cared for by a Christian family. She stood steadfast in her support of Yun's ministry and in her faith.

Their story is truly remarkable and a testimony to their tremendous faith. The last time he was imprisoned in China, his legs were badly smashed, and he was crippled from a beating. Even though he could not walk and was behind three iron doors with six armed guards, he believed God when God told him three times that he was to try to escape.

Yun says, "I have learned that when the Lord tells us to do something, there is no time for discussion, regardless of the situation we face. When we are sure that God has told us to act, as I was on this occasion, blind obedience is called for. Not to obey God implies that we are wiser than him, and that we know better how to run our lives than he does." [158]

Despite all odds, he escaped and regained full use of his legs. Currently, they are exiled in Germany. Because he escaped from prison, he can never return to China. His book, *The Heavenly Man*,[159] is a testimony of a man and a woman with tremendous faith. As I read through that book, I was constantly amazed by their faith. It made me realize how far I have to go in my faith walk.

---

[158] Brother Yun, The Heavenly Man, Monarch Books, 2002, p. 255
[159] Ibid

The picture below was taken as we stood in amazement looking at the Great Wall of China. Begun in the early 700's, and added to many times, this wall was built to protect borders.

Parts of the wall still stand after many centuries. How like our faith this is. Practices have changed, but the basic tenets remain the same. The faith of Christian believers has stood the test of time for the past 2,000 years.

What can you and I do to strengthen our faith? I hope this book has given you some thoughts to ponder. As I have written it, I have realized places where I still need to strengthen my faith. Again, that is why this book was written and called and *Upward Climb toward Faith*. It is not just an easy walk, but an arduous climb taken one step at a time.

We have each been given many talents by our creator. How are we using those talents? In the parable of the talents, [160]Jesus tells of three servants entrusted with the master's money. The first was given five bags of gold and he wisely doubled it. The second was given two bags of gold and he doubled it. The third just buried the one bag that he was given. To both men who doubled the money the master said, "Well done, good and faithful servant.

You have been faithful with a few things; I will put you in charge of many things. Come and share your master's happiness." [161] The third man was banished and told to give up what he had buried and hidden away. Unlike the third man, we need to utilize the talents we have been given. This is a phrase that we all want to hear from God, "Well done, good and faithful servant."

How will you finish your race? It is time to get on with it, because we never know when our race will end, and we will cross that final finish line. Is there something God is calling you to do? It is different for each of us, but only you can do what God has called you to do. You might be the only one who can do whatever God is asking you to do. What if you do not do it and it never gets done?

Ask what he wants you to do. Do not be fearful. Who knows? You might even end up writing a book!

---

[160] *NIV,* Matthew 25:14 – 30
[161] *Ibid,* Matthew 25:23

Respond to that call today and may he bless you richly in your endeavors. I pray this book has been a blessing to you. Writing it has been a great blessing to me. And finally, I want to leave you with this ancient blessing from the book of Numbers.

The blessing says,

> "May the LORD bless you
> and keep you;
> the LORD make his face shine on you
> and be gracious to you;
> the LORD turn his face toward you
> and give you peace."[162]

Now, you go and be a blessing to someone else!

---

[162] *Ibid,* Numbers 6:24-26

About the Author

Jackie is an accomplished author, speaker, marathoner, and optimal health coach with tremendous success as an entrepreneur. She earned a B.S, at Mami University and a M.S, from Purdue University. After teaching in a classroom for a few years, she found her true calling as an entrepreneur. She owned and operated Splashtime Swim School School for twenty years and served on the National Council of Sigma Kappa Sorority for ten years. It was then that she became known for her positive upbeat attitude.

Currently, she is the founder and CEO of Phillips Wellness Enterprises. She first published as a co-author in Team Referral Network's Collaborative Book, *Elevate,* and is co-author, again of another Team book releasing this summer entitled, *Tenacious.* Her stand-alone book, *Step by Step, 21 Steps to Enhance the Winner in You* was published in 2019.

Known for her positive attitude, Jackie was awarded the Leadership Success Summit's Upside Thinker Award in 2015. She is a member of Team Referral Network, the Riverside Chamber of Commerce, the Inland Empire Chapter of California Writers, and the Grove Community Church.

Jackie and her college sweetheart, Dick reside in Riverside, CA. They have one daughter, Nikki, and two grandkids, Haidyn and Cole. Jackie is available to speak at your next business, health-related or church event.

These are her favorite speaking Topics:
-Treating Your Body as a Holy Temple
-Faith
-Aging Gracefully
-Step by Step, Enhancing the Winner in You

-Called to Witness (Workshop)

Connect with Jackie via e-mail or social media.

E-mail- cjackiephillips@gmail.com

Website- http://www.phillips4wellness.com/

Facebook- http://www.facebook.com4jackiephillips/

LinkedIn- https://www.linkedin.com/in/jackiephillips1/

Made in the USA
Middletown, DE
25 June 2021